KENT
CHURCHES

1996

This book is dedicated to Tim Scott,
my companion on many memorable church visits

KENT
CHURCHES

JOHN E. VIGAR

Foreword by Sir Harry Secombe CBE

Photography by Colin Bourner

ALAN SUTTON PUBLISHING LIMITED

First published in the United Kingdom in 1995
Alan Sutton Publishing Limited
Phoenix Mill · Far Thrupp · Stroud · Gloucestershire

British Library Cataloguing in Publication Data

A catalogue record for this book is available from the British Library.

ISBN 0-7509-0915-3

Cover picture: Birchington, All Saints, from the south-west.

Typeset in 11/13 Baskerville
Typesetting and origination by
Alan Sutton Publishing Limited.
Printed in Great Britain by WBC Limited, Bridgend.

Contents

Acknowledgements

The author wishes to extend his sincere thanks to the following:

Sir Harry Secombe CBE, Colin Bourner, The Council for the Care of Churches, The Churches Conservation Trust, The Historic Churches Preservation Trust, The Rt Hon. The Earl of Guilford, and the Incumbents and Churchwardens of all the churches included in this book for their kindness and encouragement throughout.

Foreword

by Sir Harry Secombe CBE

I had the pleasure of sailing up the Medway with John Vigar when he did a *Highway* programme from Aylesford. We got on like a house on fire – so it was just as well that we were on the water at the time!

I was a choirboy from the age of seven until I went off to war and all the social activity of our community centred around the church and the church hall. My happiest memories of those days are of lusty hymn singing, the sight of the church Harvest Festival full to the brim with farm produce and flowers and the wonder and excitement of early Communion on Christmas morning.

The church formed the background to our lives; its bells summoned us imperiously to prayer, rang out joyfully for our weddings and tolled sadly for our passings.

Since those days churches have never ceased to fascinate me and *Highway* gave me the opportunity to visit and explore them all over the land.

I am particularly impressed by John's book because it is so well researched and illustrated. It is a wonderful guide to the ecclesiastical buildings of Kent and John's experience as a historian makes us see them in a new light, telling us what to look out for and teaching us how to appreciate the devotion and divine inspiration of those who built them. His scholarship lightens the gloom of some church architecture and provides the answers to many of its puzzling aspects. Did you know, for example, that in the thirteenth century stained glass was seen as a way to put across stories from the bible and was known as the 'poor man's bible'; or that sometimes an iron bracket next to the pulpit held an hourglass for timing the preacher's sermon? It might be a good idea to bring those back!

There is a wealth of knowledge in this book and it brings to sparkling life what in other hands might be considered a somewhat dry subject. I recommend it to everybody.

Harry Secombe
London SW1, May 1995

Preface

Churches have always been the centre of village life. Sometimes this is in both a physical and social sense, while at other locations the isolated church building may be little used but still much loved by those living in the parish. In his generous Foreword Sir Harry recalls his childhood memories of church life – remembering what went on in the building more than the structure itself. As we grow up we begin to look at the building, to put the worship in its setting, and to ask questions about how, when and why the building developed into the structure we see today.

Even the less religious among us visit old churches and recognize their importance to the history of the area. If we persevere and search out the key, the churches of Kent can offer us a wealth of detail and interest covering over 1,500 years of building history. We are particularly lucky in the variety of churches our county offers, and we need never say 'We've seen it all before'. There is no such thing as a typical church, for while they all have a similar skeleton it is in the individual differences that their interest lies.

This book explains the development of Anglican churches using specific Kent buildings as examples, and then provides a gazetteer of over two hundred worthwhile churches in the county, providing something for all tastes, be it medieval wall paintings, nineteenth-century brickwork or seventeenth-century monuments. If your local church is not featured in this book it does not mean it is of no worth – merely that my selection has been made according to specific features, and if the choice is biased at all it is towards the churches that others usually choose to ignore!

Today's visitor will find the majority of Kent churches locked, or open only at very limited hours. In order to avoid a wasted journey it is always worth looking up the incumbent's telephone number in Crockford's Clerical Directory (available in every reference library) and calling in advance. When visitors take this trouble – and by doing so show their genuine interest – they will invariably be accorded a warm welcome and given every facility.

PART 1

What to look for in a church

It was the late Sir John Betjeman who likened the study of ancient churches to reading a good detective story. No matter which part of the building we study there are always clues to be discovered. These range from the obvious, such as blocked windows and doors, to less noticeable features like the courses of construction in the walls. When we have discovered and recognized all the clues we are a little nearer to understanding how the church may have evolved – and it is up to us to solve the clues in the best way we can. It all comes with practice – and the more churches we visit the easier the process becomes. Eventually it is possible to glance at a church and assess its main features in a matter of seconds – but there is always something new to see and every church will contain something that is almost impossible to solve, keeping even the most experienced church-crawlers on their toes!

The most important study involves the ground plan of the church. If we understand how churches grew in size, the other pieces of the architectural puzzle will fit together so much more easily. It is no use looking at the fittings inside if we do not fully understand the walls that contain them.

The first country churches, built during the Saxon and Norman periods, were constructed with nave and chancel only. For this reason they are normally referred to as 'two-cell' churches. The chancel may have had a square or rounded east end. If it was rounded it would have slightly increased its size, forming a portion known as an apse. There are a few early apses in Kent, but most have disappeared as the result of later rebuilding works.

In a two-cell building the proportions were usually constant with the chancel being half the length of the nave. Sometimes there was an internal arch, separating the two rooms, and from the outside the chancel is usually seen as a slightly lower building than the nave. All early churches in Kent would have been thatched – with very steeply pitched roofs to throw the water off. No Anglican church in Kent is now roofed in this material because over the centuries more durable materials such as tile and slate have been substituted.

The church at Paddlesworth near Snodland retains its original two-cell plan, and is a good starting point for anyone wishing to study the development of church plans. Once the two-cell church has been recognized, it is often possible to pick out the original layout within most medieval churches, even though there may be no early walls or features left after subsequent rebuildings.

In the natural progression of a two-cell church the first change is most likely to have occurred during the late twelfth or early thirteenth century, when the chancel was often doubled in length to allow for a much more elaborate ritual. Sometimes you may still be able to pick out the vertical join in the stonework occasioned by this extension. At the same time an aisle was often added to the nave by cutting through either the north or south wall and adding a lean-to construction. There is nothing symbolic in the positioning of this addition; like most structural features of the medieval period it was put on the most convenient side of the building.

Incidentally, an aisle is an architectural term referring to an extension, and should never be applied to the gangway between the pews. It would have to be a very strange church indeed for the bride to 'walk down the aisle'.

DARENTH. The east wall shows characteristic Norman windows, an inset flint cross and blocked windows that served the space over the vaulted ceiling. Blocked arches to a south chapel may also be seen.

In these early churches there were no seats, except possibly a few stone benches around the walls. The aisles were added to allow for processions and side altars and not to increase seating capacity, for very rarely does the size of a church reflect the size of population. The early aisles are always very narrow structures, often no more than 6 ft wide internally. Good examples may be seen at Crundale near Wye and Harty on the Isle of Sheppey. Following the successful addition of a single aisle the decision was often made to add another on the opposite side of the nave. Because Kent was a fairly wealthy county in the fourteenth and fifteenth centuries, much rebuilding took place during these periods. By this time seating had been introduced, so these later aisles were built on a larger scale to allow for this, and often have their own roof structures. Occasionally, as at Aylesford, East Peckham Old Church and Lynsted, they are the same size as the original nave!

As we look at churches and read guidebooks we encounter a variety of architectural terms that may confuse the casual visitor. I recommend the simplified system suggested in the nineteenth century by Thomas Rickman as the only required information:

Saxon	Pre-1066
Norman Romanesque	1066–1200
Early English Gothic	1200–1300
Decorated Gothic	1250–1350
Perpendicular Gothic	1350–1530

There is, of course, a wide overlap between one period and the next with remote places adopting new styles or techniques considerably later than other areas. However, once these styles have been identified they will allow the visitor a much greater understanding of the growth of church buildings.

It must be realized that features in walls are not to be used on their own as a means of dating the church. New features have often been added to old walls, in the same way that people have replacement windows in their homes today. The study of old churches is one of putting together *all* the clues to come to an overall understanding of their history.

One of the most interesting features of the exterior is the main door. Though many smaller churches used a centrally placed door in the western wall, an equal number had a door either north or south of the nave. This would have been on the side nearest the village, and is often a good indicator of where a (now) deserted village was once located. In the fourteenth or fifteenth century as part of the general rebuilding, a door was occasionally let into the wall opposite the main door. This was not to get more people in, but

HIGHAM OLD CHURCH. A detail of the fourteenth-century south door, showing the wonderful carving of faces and geometric designs that is more than the work of some provincial craftsman.

to allow for processions which were then a major part of the liturgy, to circumnavigate the church and churchyard. It is surprising what lengths some churches went to, for at Wrotham the tower formed the western churchyard boundary and to allow processions to go round the outside of the church without leaving the churchyard a vaulted passageway was cut through the base of the tower.

Towers are a study in themselves. Occasionally we come across a massive Norman tower which dwarfs its church. Kent has examples at Milton, Leeds and Brabourne. In south-east England they were never built for defensive purposes, and often not even to hold bells. It seems that the majority were built to house the church valuables, or sometimes the priest, and also to be symbolic of pointing to heaven.

The positioning of towers at the west end of the church is traditional, and may originate in the fact that they were often added on to existing buildings.

To avoid problems with settlement they would have been built as free-standing structures, a few inches away from the existing wall. After a period of settlement they were then joined up to the main church. There are many examples in the county of short lengths of walling joining tower to church. Where the two were built joined at the same time the tower has often settled much lower and cracks have developed. The majority of western towers in Kent are heavily buttressed to guard against collapse – and none more so than Woodchurch where the buttresses are nearly as wide as the tower itself.

In East Anglia, where there is a shortage of building stone, the flint towers are round; as they do not have corners there was no need to import expensive stone from elsewhere to make the edges. In Kent we had round towers, but the last to survive, at Ospringe, fell in the seventeenth century. An example of the clumsy appearance of a square flint tower without proper stone dressings can be seen at West Kingsdown where the tower dates from the eleventh century.

Several churches had central towers between nave and chancel, but for all those that survive many others have collapsed completely. Two twelfth-century examples that survive are St Clement's at Sandwich, and Northbourne. There is a Norman example of unique style at Brook where a chapel is situated high in the tower in a fashion that may be found on the continent, but nowhere else in this country.

Many towers were originally quite short structures of two storeys, but in the fifteenth century as the ringing of bells became commonplace the bells were mounted on wheels in order to be able to turn them, and taller towers were required. It is very easy to see the new top storey on several Kent towers.

Having observed the general shape and plan of the church it is necessary to take a detailed look at the building. The first thing to notice is the material of which it is constructed. Usually in Kent it is rubble, consisting of ragstone or flint pieces as they came from the ground. Unless the church has been rendered or over-restored it should be possible to detect the stages in which it was built. Often it took many seasons to build a church and before each winter the workmen capped their unfinished wall with mortar to protect it from frost damage. By careful inspection of the walls it is possible to count the number of 'building lifts' between these horizontal layers. By this method it is possible to determine the number of seasons' work it took to construct that particular section of wall. It is common to find that each season's work resulted in the construction of about 3 or 4 ft of wall. These patterns are so easy to see today – but originally they would have been invisible as the rubble churches were invariably rendered with plaster and then painted white. The plaster has subsequently fallen off and not been replaced.

WEST KINGSDOWN. The church in the woods, built in the Saxo-Norman period with quoins of local flints. The blocked arch originally led to an apsidal tower chapel, such as still exists at Godmersham.

It is also possible, by examining the walls, to detect the lengthening of the chancel. This can be seen in the form of a vertical line on the north or south wall of the chancel – often with the former cornerstone still in situ. Sometimes the church has been reduced in size, with rows of blocked arches surviving to indicate the position of the former extensions. At Chalk, Burham and Monkton, there are excellent examples of demolished aisles being represented by very clear blocked arcades.

The south wall of the chancel is often the most interesting part of the building to study, as it contains many features of note, both inside and out. Here may be found the priest's doorway, which is usually of fourteenth- or fifteenth-century date, inserted at a time when the status of priests was at its peak.

Next to the priest's door may be a LOW SIDE WINDOW. These are popularly known as lepers' windows, although there is strong evidence that

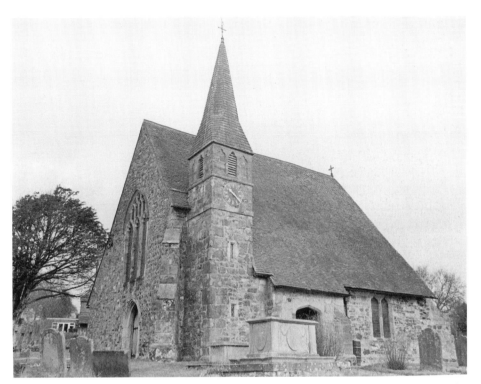

NEWENDEN. A fragment of a much larger medieval church which was given extra character in 1859 by the addition of a spirelet.

lepers were not allowed into the environs of the church. In the majority of cases low side windows were used to ring a handbell at the consecration of the host. This would tell those who were not able to attend mass that the holiest part of the service had been reached. These windows were always set into the side of the chancel that faced the village, and are another useful clue when the village itself has disappeared. If the church had a bell tower or steeple this would have been used for the sanctus bell, but the majority of churches did not have these in the early years. The bell would have been rung by a kneeling priest, thus accounting for its usual low position near the floor. It can take the form of a small window low down on its own, as at Smarden, or an ordinary window which is lengthened, like that at Hartley near Dartford.

The east wall is usually the one which contains the most magnificent window, as since the Norman Conquest it has been the focus of attention, being over the high altar. Inside we are often dazzled by the display of stained glass, but outside we are able to appreciate the design of the window itself. It

STONE. The chancel arch of this exciting thirteenth-century church is embellished with Purbeck marble shafts. The glass in the east window is of 1860 and was designed by Wailes of Newcastle.

is also only from the outside that we can discover whether the stonework is medieval or a nineteenth-century replacement. In its simplest form the east window is an arrangement of one, two or three small openings, as at West Farleigh and Bonnington. As the thirteenth century dawned these round-headed windows gave way to larger pointed windows known as lancets. This was the period when most churches could afford glass for the first time, and were able to abandon the old wooden shutters and small openings in favour of larger, protected, windows. These lancets can be in pairs, threes or fives, the larger groups rising in height to the centre. As these single lancets were placed close together they were covered with a single hood mould to throw water away from the precious glass. This gave extra areas of protected wall between windows and hood mould which could be pierced with small windows, and traceried lights came into being. At first these formed what is known as Y tracery – as can be seen in the west window at Warehorne – then more complicated designs were developed that allowed little straight-sided lights to be built into the canopy. It is windows of this, Perpendicular, period that survive in most Kent churches, as they were constructed at a time when the county was particularly wealthy following developments in the agricultural system.

Generally the north walls of both chancel and nave are the least disturbed parts of the church. This is no doubt due to the fact that throughout history the north side always represented the darker side of life and superstition even meant that it was rarely used for burials during the Middle Ages. Here, if anywhere, will be found the unrestored windows – all the others having been replaced by the Victorians who wanted the church to look pretty from the main path! It is also worth looking out for GRAFFITI on the north wall. Where dressed stone forms the corners of door and window frames, these smooth areas offered ample scope for those who could not afford proper memorials to leave their marks. The churches of Chillenden and Barfrestone both have wonderful examples, while at Capel le Ferne DV 1739 is carved on the NE corner of the chancel. A specialist type of graffito – the incised crosses left by crusaders and pilgrims – may be found in churches that were on regular travellers' routes: both Stodmarsh and Kenardington in the east of the county have excellent examples.

One of the more common exterior features of our churches is the MASS DIAL. During the Middle Ages these were used to determine the times of mass. They can usually be found on the south wall, more often than not next to one of the doors. They look like small circular sundials, with a hole in the centre where a gnomon might be inserted. The early ones had just four time lines marked within the circle, but later on these were increased to seven as the number of services per day was increased. The best preserved mass dials are to be found where a porch has been added to an early doorway, making the sundial obsolete but ensuring its preservation. Swingfield parish church shows the remains of two.

But to return to the north side of the church; just occasionally one comes across something unusual, such as a priest's house or anchorite's cell. Such a structure may be found at Molash where a small room is built abutting the tower, only entered from the nave. If it had been a vestry it would have been built adjoining the chancel, and not at the west end. A similar, although much larger, structure may be found on the south side of the tower at Ulcombe.

Anchorites' cells were usually very small lean-to buildings in which holy men and women were enclosed to devote their lives to prayer. They were inevitably built next to the chancel from where a window would have given them a permanent view of the altar. They existed at Cliffe and at Staplehurst (both on the north side of the chancel) but only their foundations may be seen today.

The ROOF COVERING is always worth looking at, as it not only tells us about the age of the roof, but adds a great deal of character to the whole. Originally all country churches would have been thatched, although Kent has no medieval churches that retain this form of cover. Tiles became more widely used during the Middle Ages and the majority of churches retain them, although some nineteenth-century restorers preferred to replace them with slate, which is quite out of character in south-east England. The visual appearance of churches like East Peckham and Wateringbury were ruined by the introduction of slate by the then diocesan architect Joseph Clarke in the last century. The delightful church at Waldershare was also made to look as though it had just dropped in from the London suburbs.

The majority of our churches stand in their own churchyards and these should be examined before one ventures inside. The oldest memorials will probably be grouped on the south and east sides of the building, fairly close to the church itself. Until the seventeenth century there were few permanent memorials, and a single churchyard cross sufficed as a communal memorial. By the middle of that century headstones started to be introduced and many churchyards in Kent show examples from that period. The geographic distribution of gravestones goes hand in hand with economic prosperity, and for this reason there may be a larger number of eighteenth- or nineteenth-century stones depending on the historical development of the area. In the Middle Ages bodies were often only interred for a few years before being discarded – to make room for new burials. This practice continued until the nineteenth century when churchyards were finally enlarged, and is the reason

IGHTHAM. William Burges designed this striking nineteenth-century tomb chest which stands to the north of the church.

for the collection of skulls and bones that forms such a macabre tourist attraction at Hythe church.

Apart from plain upright headstones one can find chest tombs of stone or brick which date from the seventeenth and eighteenth centuries. A popular local variation in Kent are the little bodystones, or lozenge-shaped slabs which were placed over the graves in the eighteenth century to discourage grave robbers.

Of the same period, but increasingly hard to find, are the rustic wooden graveboards which were placed lengthways along the grave. They were traditionally constructed from the headboard of the deceased's bed, although the well-known surviving examples at Hawkinge and Cowden were obviously purpose built.

Nineteenth- and twentieth-century churchyard memorials vary considerably in quality. The medievalist William Burges designed a tomb chest at Ightham, while the Arts and Crafts designer Henry Wilson did a whole set at Kemsing in the early 1900s. At Stansted the monument to the Waterlow family is a great piece of bravado – in the same vein as the nearby war memorial on the village green.

11

Also to be found in country churchyards are MOUNTING BLOCKS used when the main mode of transport to church was horseback. There are nice examples at Fairfield, Ightham and East Peckham. The latter also boasts a stable, where the horses were offered shelter and food during the three-hour-long services. It still contains the stalls above which are painted the names of the local gentry who were able to make use of them.

By the time we have walked around the exterior we should have a good idea of how the building evolved, the materials of which the church is built, the periods in which the local population was wealthy, and how drastically the nineteenth century affected the building. From the monuments outside we know if there were prominent local families, and from the size of the churchyard we can tell the approximate population at any given time. Now it is necessary to venture inside to compare the information given there with that we have noted outside.

As soon as we enter a church, be it large or small, the chances are that the fabric of the building itself takes second place to the furnishings. This is why it is so important to walk around the exterior first. Often we are confronted by a sea of nineteenth-century pews which destroy the medieval character of the building, which would originally have been open and relatively bare.

Throughout the history of our churches the distinction between nave and

IWADE. The original fourteenth-century door handle. The pointed tails of the two winged lizards may just be picked out.

chancel has been the most important internal feature. Even in churches which could not afford a chancel arch there would have been a screen and loft dividing the two. The screen was usually of wood, with panelling at the base, open tracery from waist to head height and a canopy above. There was usually a hinged double door in the centre, linking nave and chancel. Either on the top of the screen or placed on a beam above was a crucifix or ROOD, which gave the screen its name. To either side of the crucifix would have been a statue of Our Lady and St John, and possibly other figures which related to the patron saint of the church. Because they were high up and in semi-darkness, lights were required to be burnt in front of these statues, either as hanging or standing lamps. Access had to be obtained to the lamps, and to facilitate this a staircase was built leading to the loft on top of the screen.

At the Reformation the statues and screens were systematically demolished, although a few escaped complete destruction. The magnificent screens still to be seen in the more remote parts of England indicate the types which might have been found in Kent five hundred years ago. Medieval rood screens may

LULLINGSTONE. An early sixteenth-century rood screen, with an early eighteenth-century balustrade added at the same time as the plaster ceiling.

still be seen at Shoreham, Lullingstone, Eastchurch and Boughton under Blean. Portions may be found at many other churches, especially in those buildings where the top half of the screen was cut down to waist height, leaving the base in situ. Lenham and West Stourmouth show typical examples of this fate.

Even where no trace of the screen itself survives there are often many clues to its original position. The most common survivor is the staircase itself, often built into the thickness of the wall. Excellent examples survive at Aylesford, Ryarsh, Challock and Snodland. At Challock the wall had to be thickened by the addition of a buttress to take the staircase, and at Snodland the position of the staircase shows us that the screen ran across the nave one bay west of the chancel arch – which is something of a rarity. In churches that had extra money available, a special rood staircase tower was built, forming an architectural feature outside, like the one at Borden near Sittingbourne. Conversely, where money was limited, temporary means of access were adopted, and at

POSTLING. The chancel showing, on the right, the cut-off ends of the beam which supported a lenten veil and a second which would have formed a prickett beam for candles.

Swingfield the sill of the south-east window of the nave was cut away to make room for a wooden ladder to be propped against the screen!

Where future finances were not so assured windows were inserted to give permanent natural light to the statues. These rood loft windows were not so common in our area, but examples may be seen at East Peckham and Capel le Ferne. The latter church has an unusual chancel screen of three stone arches, with prominent corbels to support the rood statues. The beam would also have been used to support a cloth veil in Lent, when traditionally the altar was hidden from view. In the north chapel of Challock is an extremely rare medieval wooden beam that would also have supported this veil. At Postling are the sawn-off ends of another long-lost example.

SEATING is an interesting study in logistics. As originally built the Norman churches had built-in seating in the form of stone benches around the inside walls. This is the origin of the saying 'the weak go to the wall', for there were no other seats in the nave. Parts of these stone benches survive at Tonge and Cliffe among other churches, but as walls were rebuilt and churches enlarged, so they were replaced by wooden seats, which began to make an appearance in the fourteenth century. The earliest pews in the county are probably those at Cooling – very roughly carved plain benches.

Pews as we know them today started to make an appearance in the seventeenth century when preaching necessitated a longer stay in church than had previously been necessary. These early pews were of the 'box' type, which had tall sides and doors to keep out the draughts, and to give some privacy to the occupants. Contemporary accounts tell us that much drinking, reading and sleeping took place behind closed doors during the long sermons! Almost without exception, larger box pews were constructed near the front of the church for the use of the major landowners and farmers. These sometimes had tables and chairs in them, and occasionally fireplaces! As part of the same furnishing campaigns, three-decker pulpits were built, with a pew at the base for the clerk to lead the services. The central section would have been occupied by the priest, while the upper deck or pulpit proper would have been used only when a sermon was required. This upper level probably did not give a view into the larger pews, but it did give a good overview of the general congregation. The Victorians disliked box pews and removed most of them, but Fairfield, Warehorne, Trottiscliffe and New Romney have good examples.

FAMILY PEWS, because they were frequently privately owned, have often survived longer than box pews. At West Peckham the pew is up a flight of steps in the north chapel, filled with palatial panelling and giving a view over the rest of the church. Architecturally speaking, the best private pew in Kent

EAST PECKHAM OLD CHURCH. The south chapel which formed the private family pew of the Twisden family and which as a consequence escaped the wholesale restoration of the church in 1857.

is at Rolvenden. It was built in 1825 by the Gybbon-Monypenny family and is complete with a table and chairs.

One step further up the social ladder from owning a private pew was owning a private chapel, and many churches had chapels built on to them, originally intended as burial places, and after the Reformation adapted as accommodation for worship. Penshurst Church has a south chapel that still serves the owners of Penshurst Place, while Birchington has the Quex Chapel, used and maintained by successive owners of the eponymous house.

Three-decker pulpits as such are in very short supply. Fairfield has a good example, as does Stelling, while two-deckers (without the clerk's desk) may be found at Brookland and Knowlton, where the entire church retains an air of grandeur and faded elegance. Where three-deckers no longer survive, they have usually been cut down and separated to form new units. The pulpit at Old Romney is a good example of what must have once been a much grander structure.

Pulpits cover many different periods and styles. The earliest may date from the fourteenth century and an example survives at Higham Old Church near Rochester. However, it is the seventeenth century that produced the finest examples, with large structures at Ryarsh, Wilmington and Teynham. Because it played such an important part in the post-Reformation service, the pulpit has often been replaced and brought up to date, most notably in the nineteenth century. Pulpits from the Victorian period vary considerably. The stone and marble ones are often very finely carved – with exceptional examples at Wrotham and Boxley. At Kilndown the pulpit is of the wall-mounted type and is based on the thirteenth-century example at Beaulieu Abbey in Hampshire, reached from a staircase in the thickness of the wall.

Kent gives a home to two redundant pulpits from Westminster Abbey. The earliest is at Trottiscliffe and was built for the abbey by Henry Keene in 1775. It has a graceful palm tree holding up the sounding board above. The second was designed by Blore in 1827 and is now to be found at Shoreham in the Darent Valley.

Once we get into the chancel we find more examples of woodwork. At Ruckinge and Ivychurch we can find medieval stalls in their original position. These are arranged to face each other in 'collegiate' fashion, with two or three stalls turned to face east. Many churches had these stalls even though they did not have the staff to use them. They were often demolished at the same time as the rood screen. Sometimes they incorporate misericords – tip-up seats – with elaborate carvings on the underside. Kent has several particularly fine sets including Maidstone, Minster in Thanet and Faversham.

A more durable form of seating is to be found in the chancel. Sedilia are stone seats, usually in a group of three, that are built into the south wall of the chancel near the high altar. They can be grouped under one arch, or more usually under a series of arches, and are as plain or as fancy as medieval finances allowed. They provided accommodation for the priest, deacon and sub-deacon, at various stages of the mass. They often add great character to this part of the church and for this reason tended to survive the nineteenth-century restorations – albeit in an 'improved' condition. In many cases the easternmost seat is higher than the other two, indicating that this was the priest's position. At Womenswold there are three seats under plain canopies, while at Preston near Faversham there are three remarkably ornate canopied seats. Sometimes a fourth arch was added to the east at a later date to take in a piscina, which will be explained later, and this juxtaposition may be seen at many Kent locations. Once you have identified a sedile there is little chance of confusing one again – except in a church where a decorative arcade has been built along the walls, as at Alkham and Cooling. When the south wall of

TROTTISCLIFFE. The enormous pulpit with palm tree sounding board which was designed for Westminster Abbey by Henry Keene in the late eighteenth century.

COOLING. A thirteenth-century double piscina, triple sedilia and extensive wall arcading make this chancel one of the most elaborate in the county.

a chancel was rebuilt the sedilia were not always replaced. Lavish churches like East Peckham and Seal almost certainly lost their sedilia as a result of church enlargements. Luckily when enlargements were planned at Upchurch and New Romney the sedilia were saved and they now serve their original purpose in an otherwise redundant piece of wall!

Even the plainest sedilia were fairly expensive and not all churches could afford them. Even so there was a need to provide permanent seating for the clergy in the chancels. In these cases a practice common in East Anglia was followed. The sill of the easternmost window in the south wall of the chancel was extended down to form a plain shelf that could serve as a seat. An ornate example of this can be found at Ashford and another at Hawkinge.

In a recent survey, one of the greatest attractions for visitors to our churches turned out to be the FONT. It is hardly surprising, as they are a feature to be found in almost every church and collectively they cover an even greater period of history than the churches themselves. Baptism – admission to church membership – has always been an important ceremony and in the

Middle Ages those who were not baptised were required to leave the church before mass was celebrated.

Because the naves of our churches were often used for secular events the font and its holy water were protected with a lockable cover. In many churches the rusty hinges, or holes in the stonework, show where these covers originally fitted. Fonts fall into several different categories, and are, like other types of furnishing, as plain or elaborate as finances of the period would allow.

The two most memorable fonts in Kent are the leaden ones dating from the Norman period at Lower Halstow and Brookland. They were cast towards the end of the twelfth century, probably in France. It is easy, therefore, to imagine their carriage by water to these two churches. It would be a study in itself to evaluate the importance of water transport for other materials and furnishings to be found in our parish churches. Many Norman stone fonts, which are relatively common, are lined with lead, but these two are solid lead. The Lower Halstow font, 12 in high, has ten arches, each covering a king and an angel. It is a repeating pattern and the joins between sections can be clearly seen. At some stage the whole font was encased in plaster and the leadwork was only uncovered in 1921 after a piece of the plaster fell off following a bomb blast.

The Brookland font is a slightly larger and more elaborate affair. As Romanesque designs grew more complicated the subjects tended to reflect

NEWENDEN. One of the largest and most elaborate Norman fonts in the county, carved with strange creatures and geometrical figures.

day-to-day lifestyles. Here there are two rows of figures – one representing the signs of the zodiac, the other the labours of the months. It is a beautiful piece of workmanship and the various figures are charming, particularly the October labour of treading grapes!

Later fonts are of stone and relatively plain. They nearly always mirror the architectural style of the period, and we can therefore follow the Romanesque through to Decorated and Perpendicular types. Some are more inventive than others; particularly pleasing is the fifteenth-century font at Farningham which is East Anglian in style and represents the seven sacraments.

Following the Reformation smaller fonts were built, partly due to the fact that the babies were no longer fully immersed in the water. The little font at Lullingstone is worthy of mention. It is made of marble and is enclosed in a little wooden wall cupboard. In stark contrast is the eighteenth-century stone font at Kenardington which is oval, and would be mistaken for a bird-bath if placed outside! It probably dates from 1717 when a new wooden screen was placed in the church.

The nineteenth century produced a variety of fonts. They often attract more attention as the carving on them is clean and crisp when compared with those of three hundred years earlier. Many Victorian fonts are intended to be copies of earlier designs, although they are not necessarily designs that had previously been used in the same church. Other nineteenth-century fonts are solely 'of their age' and may be found at Kingsdown, St Faith Maidstone and Sts Peter and Paul Dover. The church at Aylesford boasts a font by John Thomas, a notable sculptor whose work may be found at Pugin's Palace of Westminster.

Near the main door into many pre-Reformation churches can be found a small niche, a foot or so high, at waist height from the floor. This is a HOLY WATER STOUP built to contain water which had been blessed by the priest. On entering and leaving the church the congregation would cross themselves with holy water. As the main door of the church has usually been rebuilt on several occasions in its history, holy water stoups have often been thrown out. If the rebuilding took place after the Reformation there was no need to retain the stoup. Those that do survive are often plain arched recesses, either inside the church, or in the main porch. Examples survive at Tonbridge (outside west door), Thurnham (north porch), Smarden (north and south doors) and Cliffe (south porch).

Another receptacle associated with water is the PISCINA. Before mass the priest would wash his fingers in this feature to be found next to every medieval altar. This niche in the wall, which resembles a holy water stoup, has a basin in the bottom with a drain in it. This drain leads through the wall of the chancel and into the churchyard. As with all types of stone carving, piscinae can be plain or elaborate. They were always constructed close to the altars, more often in a south wall. Sometimes, after the sedilia were built there was little room left for the piscina which had to be squeezed in at an awkward angle. At Warehorne it juts out obliquely. In the medieval church there were often many side altars, in aisles and chapels, and to facilitate the mass at them they each had a piscina. In exceptional circumstances a parish church may have had thirteen altars! After the Reformation these side altars were removed, leaving the piscinae as sole reminders that an altar ever existed in this part of the church. These redundant piscinae may be found in many Kent churches including East Peckham and Waldershare.

In many churches there are HAGIOSCOPES cut through the walls to allow the priests at side altars to have a view of the main altar. Mass was often said at several altars at the same time and these internal 'windows' allowed the service to be coordinated. Many churches still mistakenly refer to these small holes in the walls as lepers' windows or squints, but lepers would never have been allowed into the medieval church. There are excellent examples of hagioscopes at Offham, Boxley, St Mary Cray and Paddlesworth near Folkestone. By standing at the high altar and looking through the hagioscope one can locate the position of the former side altar that it served. These were usually at the east ends of aisles, or in front of the rood screen to either side of the chancel arch.

OFFHAM. The thirteenth-century chancel arch was set within the original Norman opening, which may be seen over the top. There are also two simple hagioscopes to north and south.

In churches that had a medieval bell tower a bell would be rung at the consecration of the host, and to allow a bell ringer to have a view of the altar a hagioscope was often cut through the wall linking tower and church. These may be seen at Boxley, Aylesford and Hernhill.

Another hole in the wall can be found in different parts of the church. This is an AUMBRY, which usually takes the form of a square or rectangular cupboard with little in the way of decoration. They may contain one or more shelves, for it was here that the holy oils used for the sacraments of baptism and confirmation were stored, together with the sacred vessels. The aumbries are usually redundant today and have lost their doors, but medieval hinges often survive, as may be seen at Chillenden. There are examples in many churches – Woodchurch has a large number, and at Paddlesworth the aumbry on the south side of the nave is made of chalk blocks which may be detected through the thickness of the wall on the outside.

In the medieval period processions played an important part in the daily

HIGHAM OLD CHURCH. The medieval aumbry in the north chapel which has managed to retain its original hinged door.

life of every church, and banners were frequently carried. These banners had to be stored in the church, and special cupboards constructed for their long poles. These are a common feature of East Anglian churches, but are not so often found in Kent. Stelling and Sandwich both show examples of these cupboards which are known as BANNER STAVE LOCKERS. They are usually found in the nave as the banners were the responsibility of the people and not the priest.

Before we leave the subject of holes in the wall we must mention a rarity – a WAFER OVEN to bake the wafers for the mass. Two churches seem to exhibit these features; Smarden has one in the chancel, while in the vestry at Otford is a further example.

Church buildings themselves could be classed as memorials to those who built them. Sir Christopher Wren's epitaph in St Paul's Cathedral tells us, 'if you seek his monument look around you'. Yet it is rare today for us to know the names of the architects, craftsmen and labourers who gave us the churches we like to visit.

From the earliest times it was considered right to bury within the precincts of the church, although this usually meant in the churchyard rather than the church itself. The Saxons allowed burial in the church for notable figures, and a little chapel – the porticus – was added to the nave to take just one burial. These soon went out of fashion and for several hundred years parish churches saw no burials within their walls. It was during the Norman period that burial within the church came back into fashion – but only for those of a certain status – and these special burials in a roundabout way lead on to the erection of monuments.

The earliest burials of notables were in solid stone coffins. These were constructed by carving a coffin shape, slicing the top off to form a lid and digging out the centre. Because of their bulk and weight they were then let into the floor of the church and the burials made into them, at which stage the lid was placed on top. This lid then lay flush with the floor of the church, which was otherwise of beaten earth. Occasionally these would be surrounded by a small area of glazed tile, but otherwise the COFFIN LID would have been the only solid feature of a very soft church floor.

The first carvings to appear on these coffin lids took the form of a plain cross. This could run the whole length of the stone, or be made up of two or three small crosses. There was no inscription, so where they survive we do not know whose coffin they covered. Examples may be seen at Brasted, Chevening, Nackington and West Malling. At Penshurst is an interesting fragment which shows a carving of a lady with hands upraised in prayer. She has a semi-smiling expression, and it may represent her reception into heaven. It is generally believed that she is a member of the Albigensian sect who fled to England in the thirteenth century after they had been outlawed by Pope Innocent III.

Before the end of the thirteenth century most coffin lids started to include a representation of the deceased person, and this rapidly led to the development of the TOMB CHEST. A portion of a thirteenth-century coffin lid with an effigy on it survives at Detling. With this carving there came an increased respect for the burial place and it was decided to raise the carved piece off the floor so that people could not walk over it. This created the tomb chest – a solid rectangular block of stone, like a table – on which the effigy could be placed. These imitated the shrines of the saints. In fact there is a most unusual early monument at Fordwich near Canterbury which looks like a little house with a tile roof and pre-dates tomb chests proper by about a hundred years. It may have originated in Canterbury Cathedral.

The tomb chest did not necessarily have an effigy on it – some would have had a plain polished top – but the majority did have some form of decoration. As artistic techniques progressed, so it was possible to elaborate on the decoration applied to the chests, which by the Tudor period were highly sculptured and coloured. While the early ones were always made of local stone, the later examples used imported alabaster and marble to produce a highly refined work of art. By the seventeenth century they had become such highly prized objects that they were even being signed by their designers and sculptors.

In the Middle Ages there was a special type of tomb chest that had a flat top, and was built to the north of the high altar. This was known as an EASTER SEPULCHRE, and for most of the year functioned as an ordinary tomb. However on Maundy Thursday the consecrated host was placed on it under a veil and until it was ceremoniously uncovered at the first mass of Easter morning this became a focus of devotion, symbolic of Christ's death and entombment. Good examples of monuments of this type may be seen at Otford and Cliffe.

But to return to monuments of the Middle Ages, the CANOPIED MONUMENT made an appearance in the late thirteenth century. It was customary in some areas to place a temporary canopy of silk over a newly dug grave, to give it some honour. Even when this honour was made permanent by the erection of a tomb chest over the top a canopy was still used, and this practice developed into the use of a permanent canopy of stone.

The earliest of these stone canopies were formed when the tomb chest was placed against a wall, and a piece of carved stone constructed to form a back. This was then carried up the wall and brought forward as an overhang, occasionally supported by pillars, but in the early days normally just a short canopy. As space was limited in the chancel these monuments were often set into the wall in a niche, with the canopy being formed within the thickness of the wall itself. My favourite example of this type of monument may be found at Ightham and commemorates Sir Thomas Cawne who died in 1374. It forms part of a unit with the window above. He is shown wearing a mixture of chain and plate mail with a dog at his feet. A slightly earlier monument of the same form is the canopied tomb of Sir Robert de Shurland at Minster in Sheppey, dating from about 1320. His legs are crossed, which the Victorians explained away as symbolic of his attendance on crusades. This explanation is completely without foundation; his legs are crossed for purely artistic reasons, to give the figure some semblance of life. Other canopied tombs remain at Sandwich, Goudhurst, Ash and Ickham.

There are also some medieval rarities. Two Kent churches contain medieval HEART SHRINES. The earlier of the two is at Leybourne and contains the heart of Sir Roger de Leybourne who was killed on crusade in 1272. In those days it was not possible to bring a body back so far for burial, and only vital organs were returned to the deceased's church. Sir Roger's heart was placed in a small stone casket which was let into the wall. It was opened by the Victorians, who were fascinated by the idea of this type of burial. The second heart shrine to survive is at Brabourne, but it is much

IGHTHAM. Sir Thomas Cawne's (d. 1374) is one of the finest monuments of its date in Kent, and was constructed at the same time as the window above.

battered and we have no idea whose heart it contains, although Aymer de Valence who died in 1296 has been suggested as a likely candidate.

By far the most discussed type of memorials are MONUMENTAL BRASSES. Kent has more of these than any other county: over 150 of our churches have at least one example. The oldest, and one of the most impressive, is at Chartham and commemorates Sir Robert de Septvans who died in 1306. It shows him full size – 6 ft 3 in tall, with a bare head and wearing a tunic over his chain mail.

The material of which these memorials is made is not brass, but an alloy known as latten, which was not made in this country. This explains why Kent, the nearest county to the continent, displays most examples. Although to us today they seem colourless and dull, they were often originally highly coloured by the use of inlaid enamels on the shields, faces and armour. The development of brasses is easily noted. As the centuries passed latten became more difficult to obtain and figures, of necessity, became much smaller, but often with this came an extra intricacy. Single figures gave way to couples, and later to children as well. After the fourteenth century the stone canopies that had become fashionable over the tomb chests shed their influence on brasses, and elaborate metal canopies were set into the stone slabs as well. Because the brasses are set into the floor they have often been damaged, or have disappeared altogether, leaving the outline of the monument as sole reminder of the person it commemorated.

The delight of our county's brasses lies in the fact that they show a wide range of figures, wearing many stylized costumes and, even if they do not include details of whom they commemorate, in terms of costume and art history they are just as useful to us, helping us to put a social scale on church history.

The best church – not just in Kent, but in England – in which to study brasses is Cobham, where the entire chancel floor is covered with large figures. They date in the main from the fourteenth and fifteenth centuries and mostly commemorate members of the de Cobham family who were prominent in national affairs throughout the Middle Ages. Most have been moved on more than one occasion, and some are more than a little restored, but the impressive display is one of the special sights of Kent.

Without doubt, the churches of Kent offer as good a selection of sixteenth- and seventeenth-century monuments as those of any other county. It is an almost impossible task to arrange them in any order, but we can classify them into three main types. The first is the familiar tomb chest, which had developed into an elaborate display of heraldry, with figures of the deceased on the top. That to Lord Brooke, 9th Lord Cobham at Cobham (erected

1561) is one of the most notable in the county and shows Lord and Lady Cobham surrounded by ten sons and four daughters. It was restored in the nineteenth century after a roof timber fell on it. From about the same date is the magnificent tomb of Sir Thomas Moyle from Eastwell. When that church became a ruin in 1952 the monument was removed to the Victoria & Albert Museum. Other monuments of the tomb chest type may be seen at Chevening, Waldershare, Southfleet and Throwley.

An alternative to the tomb chest is the STANDING WALL MONUMENT, where an effigy would be carved under an elaborate canopy that was let into the wall. This is the later development of the canopied wall monument popular in the fourteenth century. Sometimes this canopy has many tiers, each tier carrying an inscription, effigy, armorial bearing or other device. A good example, from 1638, may be found on the south side of the chancel at Ightham, while at Lullingstone you can see just how far the sculptor could go when allowed, on Sir Percival Hart's monument! By far the best example of this type of monument may be found at Otterden where it was carved by Epiphanius Evesham who also worked in other nearby churches. In the east of the county at Northbourne an equally interesting standing wall monument to Sir Edwin Sandys – one of the first settlers in the American state of Virginia – may be found.

The third type of monument, the HANGING WALL MONUMENT, was introduced in the Elizabethan period, and became widespread by the end of the sixteenth century. These are similar in design to standing wall monuments, except that they do not touch the floor; they hang on the wall in the way one would hang a picture. It is this form of memorial which has continued to be used to the present day – helped on its way by the introduction in the early part of the seventeenth century of imported marbles, to replace the decreasing supplies of coloured alabaster. At the end of the sixteenth century alabaster reserves were becoming very stained, which was most unsuitable for effigies. In order to overcome the staining effigies were highly painted. In West Malling church the effigy of Sir Robert Brett, which has recently been repainted, shows how bright a painted alabaster memorial would have looked when it was newly erected.

To start with the hanging monument often mimicked its standing counterpart in so far as it showed a representation of the deceased – sometimes a full figure in miniature, at other times head and shoulders only. Among the grand selection of monuments at Ightham is that to Dame Dorothy Selby who died in 1641. It shows her bust set against representations of two pieces of her needlework. Dame Dorothy was for some time supposed to have been associated with the discovery of the Gunpowder Plot, for the

IGHTHAM. The standing wall monument to Sir William Selby (d. 1638). To the left is the more famous memorial to Dorothy Selby, who died in 1641, her bust carved by Edward Marshall.

inscription is ambiguously worded. However, current thinking is that it tells the reader about her needlework, rather than about any other achievements.

At Bishopsbourne, a similar hanging monument commemorates Richard Hooker, and to provide a contrast the mid-seventeenth-century example at Birchington to the Crispe family shows six small busts combined into one memorial.

The most common form of hanging wall monument did not include an effigy of any kind, but just showed an inscription. These tablets always followed the architectural styles of the day and are mainly classical or baroque in influence. By the eighteenth and nineteenth centuries they had become relatively inexpensive and this accounts for the vast number that survive.

One of the most impressive seventeenth-century monuments in Kent is to Sir John Banks (d. 1699) at Aylesford. It shows Sir John, his wife and son, dressed in Roman attire. Above them cherubs carry swags to a height of 30 ft. In complete contrast the free-standing monument to Sir Henry Furnesse (d. 1712) at Waldershare is a wedding-cake-like structure, which rises in tiers until it is so high that it is difficult to see the top. It was erected in a purpose-built brick chapel added to the north of the chancel. The figures at the base of the monument represent broken-hearted ladies, but today they have broken noses and arms as well! The church is no longer used and is cared for by the Earl of Guilford.

Another free-standing marble monument is that to the Oxenden family at Wingham. It was erected in 1682 and is surrounded by contemporary black and white tile flooring. The design on the monument is one of black ox heads, white cherubs and garlands of flowers hanging off a tall pinnacle.

In the delightful church of Knowlton, owned by the Churches Conservation Trust, are two monuments which appear to be a pair. On closer inspection they are quite different. The earlier commemorates Sir John Narborough and his brother who were lost when Sir Cloudesley Shovell's ship, the *Association*, went down off the Isles of Scilly in 1707. On the front is a marvellous relief of the ship on the rocks, while the inscription above relates the tragic loss of these two young men. Opposite, and in complete contrast, is the memorial of 1721 to Lady D'Aeth, which is something of an anti-climax, having all the simplicity of a Victorian washstand.

There are other reminders of death in our churches. During the sixteenth and seventeenth centuries FUNERAL ARMOUR was made to be carried at the funerals of important people. These helmets, swords and gauntlets were made of cheap metal and placed on the coffin as it made its way to the church. They were then hung over the place of burial as a symbol of respect. In recent

KNOWLTON. The naval scene on the base of
the marble monument to Sir John
Narborough. He died in 1707 when his ship,
the *Association*, went down off the Isles of Scilly.

years the few remaining examples have nearly all been stolen, and the others
removed for safety, but the church at Aylesford still has a representative
selection.

As the custom of carrying funeral armour died out, it was replaced by a
new status symbol, the HATCHMENT. This was a coat-of-arms painted on a
large framed canvas that showed the achievements of the deceased person.
These had the advantage that the heraldry often showed the lineage of the
person, and because of their decorative nature they often ended up as
permanent fittings in the church. Otford has a veritable gallery of them, while
many other churches have at least one or two examples. One at Bilsington
dates from as late as 1945.

Although there are many thousands of eighteenth- and nineteenth-century
tablets, there are few large monuments in the churches from these periods. At
Linton is the remarkable monument to Viscount Brome dating from 1835. It
depicts the 22-year-old man lying on a couch, the sheet that covers him
falling surprisingly naturally. In comparison a slightly earlier monument at
Chevening to Lady Frederica Stanhope (d. 1827) on a similar couch is much
more moving. She died in childbirth and is shown suckling her infant. For a
brief period after 1890 large monuments came back into fashion and that at
Crockham Hill to Octavia Hill (d. 1912), founder of the National Trust, is a
good example.

The floors of our churches can be treasure-houses for those seeking LEDGER STONES. These are large stone slabs that carry inscriptions, but which do not necessarily cover the grave. During the nineteenth century restorations meant that the floors of our churches were usually relaid. This resulted in the loss of many ledger stones, so when you walk into a church and find them surviving they are always worth studying. Graveney, Fordwich, Brookland and Warehorne are all excellent examples where the ledgers are separated by uneven groups of red tiles, bricks and stone flags. In west Kent there is an unusual type of ledger, made of cast iron, indicating the proximity of the Wealden iron industry. Just over the border into Sussex there are large groups (particularly at Wadhurst), but in Kent they are usually found singly. Because they are very heavy it was not possible to carry them long distances, so they remained confined to the areas of their manufacture. If they carry an inscription letters are often found back to front, as they had to be cast in reverse! The furthest one from the centre of the iron industry is in the old church at East Peckham, and rather unusually shows a plain cross with an inset inscription in brass.

These, then, are the major types of purpose-built monument to be found in our churches, but there are many other ways in which people have been commemorated. Most forms of furnishing dating from the nineteenth and twentieth centuries have been given in memory of loved ones and will usually carry an inscription to that effect.

Since the Reformation ROYAL ARMS showing the monarch's achievement have been placed in churches to show the monarch's position as head of the church. There are few early survivors, because most were ordered to be removed during the Commonwealth period (1649–60). At Westerham is the earliest example in Kent (one of the earliest anywhere) dating from the reign of Edward VI (1547–53), and Charing has the arms of Charles I (1625–49). Following the Restoration of Charles II in 1660 all Anglican churches were ordered to display a royal arms, and most subsequent monarchs are represented in the county. The following are representative examples: Charles II – Ashford, James II – West Malling, William and Mary – Acrise, Anne – Preston next Wingham, George I – Chiddingstone, George II – Cranbrook, George III – Brook.

With the exception of some of the Romney Marsh churches most Kent churches contain at least fragments of STAINED GLASS. The practice of glazing church windows started in the late seventh century when artists came to northern England from Gaul. From the start there was controversy as to its suitability, and as late as the twelfth century St Bernard of Clairveaux said that too much ornament in a church took men's minds from spiritual things. The earliest glass to be found in Kent is usually GRISAILLE, a lightly patterned glass often used high up where figures could not be seen. Medieval examples may be seen at Snodland, Chartham and Bekesbourne. There is some very early glass at Brabourne, dating from the twelfth century. It has a bold design of circles, with little flowers in between, painted in bright reds, greens and gold. It may well be the oldest glass in its original window anywhere in Kent, although it was releaded in the nineteenth century.

By the thirteenth century patterned glass had been replaced by painted, allowing figures to be incorporated in the design. An early use of this form of glazing was the Jesse window, which resembled Christ's family tree, with branches rising heavenwards with figures standing on each one. Two good examples of this interesting concept are at Westwell and Nackington.

As the thirteenth century drew to a close there developed a greater awareness of preaching, and windows were used to put bible stories across – leading to the term 'poor man's bible'. It is so much easier for us to remember something we can see, rather than just hear about, and at a time when most people had no access to books and few could read windows played an important part in our understanding of things religious.

KEMSING. The remarkable screen rebuilt in the late nineteenth century and embellished with Comper's typical figures. It shows how most medieval churches would have looked five hundred years ago.

Glass from the fourteenth century can be found in many Kent churches, although hardly ever in its complete state. Most windows of this period represented either single figures or pairs of figures – Our Lady or the Virgin and Child being the most popular representations, the former surviving in the church at Stowting. There is a pleasant Christ in Majesty at West Kingsdown, while the east window at Selling, of about 1300, is exceptionally fine, with the bold and colourful figures set into grisaille glass.

Most human figures were painted with an elaborate canopy over the top, to fit into the tracery of the window, and even where the main figures have been lost or destroyed, the canopies often survive, and may be found at East Malling, Trottiscliffe and East Peckham. There are many other churches that show assemblages of medieval fragments: Meopham, Brabourne and Teynham display good examples.

The sixteenth century saw the destruction, occasioned by the Reformation, of many fine windows. There is, therefore, little in the way of stained glass from this period. At Iwade is a rare early sixteenth-century window of the Crucifixion. It may well represent the completion of building works on the church that commenced in 1504. At West Wickham is a parallel example where Sir Henry Heydon had the church extended and improved in the fifteenth century, again marking completion of the work by inserting stained glass. In this particular church the glass was probably designed by Flemish artists who were settling in London. If so, it marks the start of a three-hundred-year period when it was foreign, and not English, glass that was consistently inserted into our churches. With only a few exceptions it was not until the early nineteenth century that English glass made a reappearance.

For the rest of the sixteenth century churches were in a state of confusion, trying to adapt to changes in religious thinking, and it was not until the seventeenth century that much was done in the way of rebuilding or refitting churches. Two Kent churches have good collections of seventeenth-century imported glass from Switzerland. At Temple Ewell are representations of Pharoah's Dream, Joseph and his sons, and the Annunciation, while at Patrixbourne are several windows of Samson and the Agony in the Garden. It must be significant that these two churches are in the east of the county, with direct communication links to the continent. There is a rare example of eighteenth-century glass at Lullingstone, designed by Peckitt of York, and installed in 1754. The designs represent St Luke and St Botolph (patron saint of the church) and show the low point to which English glass design had descended since the Reformation.

It was in the nineteenth century that the art of stained glass design and manufacture started to improve, and the demand created by the wholesale reordering of our churches, together with the erection of new ones, was difficult to satisfy. One of the earliest Kent windows of the nineteenth century is the south chancel window at West Stourmouth. It is very deep gold and shows St Peter surrounded by a lovely vine leaf border, and dates from about 1838.

Sometimes whole churches were reglazed in a single scheme (Aylesford has twelve windows of 1878), but most churches have a wide selection of different dates and styles. Occasionally this new glass tried to recreate medieval designs, but more often interpreted them in modern fashion. The set at Acrise of 1855 is very dark and overly bold, but fits together very well and should be inspected by those wishing to get a good overview of Victorian glass.

Among the best-known glass workshops of the period was Morris and Co., whose work can be found at Speldhurst and Langton Green. Dating mainly from the 1870s they represent single figures and groups rather than biblical scenes. At St Stephen, Tonbridge, you can see glass by the same firm, but it dates from the twentieth century and has lost much of the early sparkle. Another workshop worth examining is that of Clayton and Bell. The 1861 east window at Bicknor is reputedly one of their best works. Of similar vintage is the east window at Sittingbourne. Clayton and Bell also mastered the art of copying older glass, which can be seen to advantage at Groombridge where a collection of seventeenth-century armorial glass is difficult to identify among the copies inserted by the firm.

In 1896 a remarkable window was erected at Wickhambreux. It is in Art Nouveau style and is stunning in its design and colouring. It is the work of the American studio of Baron Arild Rosenkrantz.

Throughout Kent may be found the work of Charles Eamer Kempe, the greatest and most prolific of Victorian stained glass designers. He was based in nearby Sussex and had lots of connections in the county. His work has a style that may easily be identified – although his success led to copying by other studios. Most Kempe windows are signed with his little wheatsheaf symbol, which after his death in 1907 had a small castellated tower, the symbol of his partner Tower, superimposed on all new commissions.

Other designers also signed their work. One of the greatest church furnishers of the twentieth century, Sir Ninian Comper, did much work in Kent, and a window in the north-east transept of Rochester Cathedral shows his little symbol – a wild strawberry plant. One of his earliest windows is at Kemsing, but this was erected before he adopted the trademark. One of his pupils was Martin Travers whose work at both Barham and Fordwich is notable. Travers always managed to combine stylistic figures with naturalistic

WICKHAMBREUX. The Art Nouveau east window, erected in 1896 by the artist Baron Arild Rosenkrantz.

trees, and his work is as popular today as that of his nineteenth-century predecessors.

The county's most famous set of twentieth century windows may be found at Tudeley. They are the work of Marc Chagall who was first commissioned to design a memorial window there in 1967. Following its unveiling he designed a complete set which today draws thousands of tourists to this pretty farmyard church.

It is worth getting a specialist book on stained glass, and ensuring you have a pair of binoculars with you when you visit churches, for it is often in the details, rather than the overall design, that our interest in stained glass really lies.

In the Middle Ages the interior walls of most of our churches were covered with MURALS. During the seventeenth century they were often whitewashed over so as not to give offence to the Puritans, and subsequently forgotten. When churches were restored in the nineteenth century the old plaster was hacked off and replaced, taking the medieval murals with it. In twenty or so Kent churches, the paintings were discovered before it was too late and restored, although they often do little for the look of a church, having faded to a dirty red colour, and being almost impossible to make out clearly. What we must understand is that these were not works of art to make the place look pretty, but rather they formed symbolic teaching aids, with every pose and gesture of significance. Almost invariably the subjects were grim – warning everyone to pay attention to their spiritual life lest they should spend a long time in purgatory.

In general the wall paintings in Kent are not well preserved. The best example is at Brookland, and shows the martyrdom of St Thomas à Becket. This mural was discovered about twenty years ago, which accounts for its good state of preservation. It shows Becket on his knees with the three knights looming over him, watched by his horrified chaplain. At Stone, near Dartford, is another, less striking, representation of the same event.

Other murals are either of biblical scenes or individual saints, and date in the main from the thirteenth and fourteenth centuries. The bible scenes are to be found at Bapchild, Brook, Capel, Faversham and Halling. Individual saints survive at Bishopsbourne, Cliffe, Doddington, Eastry and Frindsbury. Occasionally we find an unusual example – at Lower Halstow is a picture of a pilgrim in a boat – surely a reference to the position of this lovely church where the river laps its churchyard wall.

Several churches show a painting of St Christopher – one of the saints associated with travel in the Middle Ages – opposite, or above, the main door. There is one at Brook and another at Borden. At Snargate is a painting of a ship which dates from the sixteenth or seventeenth century and which by tradition would have told smugglers that the parson knew of a hiding place for their contraband should they need a safe haven in a hurry! In all probability this theory was invented by the Victorians to explain away a feature for which they could find no logical explanation.

In the lovely churches of the Marsh, and nearby, are the famous TEXT BOARDS, painted during the eighteenth and nineteenth centuries when there was a definite bias towards biblical texts and scriptures. The text boards were usually oval or rectangular in shape, 2 ft or so across, and painted in black and white. They are an essential ingredient in the Marsh churches – almost as important as the plain glass in their windows – and may be found at Fairfield, Brenzett, Bilsington, Warehorne and Ivychurch among others.

Another type of painted board is the BENEFACTION BOARD. From the sixteenth century, and sometimes earlier, local landowners left single fields to provide an income for the benefit of the poor. The best-known example in Kent is the Bread and Cheese lands at Biddenden left by the famous Siamese twins whose picture stands on the village green. The charity still continues, even though the original land has been developed. Some villages had many bequests of this type and to keep a record of them, as well as to perpetuate the name of the donor, boards were commissioned to record them. There are few churches that do not display them, although all too often they date from after the Tithe Act of 1836 when odd, unaccounted-for acres of land came to light as a result of government legislation. Some of the benefactions were straightforward, consisting of small amounts of money, bread and scholarships, but some boards provide us with a deeper view of social life in previous centuries.

At Snodland church the boards record 'the purchase of Great Coats for such poor persons being inhabitants'. Stone in Oxney has a field still called 'Poor Man's Field' which provides the original 13s 4d per year as stipulated in John Style's will of 1556!

Next to the benefaction boards at Fordwich are two BREAD SHELVES where the charity loaves were placed before distribution. A similar custom existed at Goudhurst where John Bathurst left an endowment to supply bread which was piled on his tomb at the back of the church. The benefaction boards, painted on leather, hang in the porch. Thomas Idenden (d. 1566) left money for the trustees of his charity at Frittenden to have an annual meal at the Bell Inn. The board at Woodchurch is dated 1774 and records three charities, that of Sir Edward Hales excluding 'all such as have been known to beg or pilfer in their youth'. St Margaret's church at Rochester has a hanging memorial to John Baynard which also gives details of his will. He left:

to his relations and friends	£20,000
to Bethlem Hospital	1,000
to the Marine Society	1,000
to the Society for the Relief of Small Debtors	1,000
to the Sunday School of St Margaret's	300
to the poor of it who do not receive alms	100

As we travel from church to church we begin to recognize the items which we have not come across anywhere else.

At Cranbrook is a DIPPING POOL, built at the top of a staircase just inside the main door. This was constructed by the Revd John Johnson in 1710 as a way of encouraging people back to the established church. The Baptists were becoming a real threat in Cranbrook and by introducing as many Baptist practices as he could get away with, Mr Johnson was trying to stabilize his decreasing congregation!

In Preston next Wingham church is a LIBRARY CUPBOARD with the inscription, 'for the use of the Vicars of Preston'. It was presented to the church by the Revd Dr Bray (1656–1730) who founded the SPCK, and was one of eighty such libraries given to help poor clergy who would not otherwise have had access to learned religious tomes.

Of the several POOR BOXES that survive in Kent, the one at Hackington is the finest. It is of the pillar type, beautifully carved, with the metal moneybox stuck on the top almost as an afterthought. It carries the inscription 'REMEMBER THE POOR', and dates from 1634.

While many of our churches display the dedication crosses that were painted on the walls of the building on the day of consecration, only one medieval church has a DEDICATION STONE. This is at Postling, and tells us that the church was dedicated 'nineteen days before the Kalends of September', which was 14 August, St Eusebius' day. What a pity the inscription did not record the year! As the stone is intact it is not a case of the inscription being lost or destroyed.

Those familiar with Norfolk will know only too well what elaborate displays of decoration may be obtained by the use of flint flushwork – the cutting of flints to show their shiny insides and their use to make patterns in the wall. In Kent we have three churches that display flint flushwork crosses. The first is at Darenth near Dartford, on the east wall of the chancel. The second is at Challock, where it may be clearly seen on the west face of the tower. It is possible that these flint crosses marked the extent of building on a special day – for instance the patronal festival. This would account for their different position in each building. The third is to be found at Eastwell.

POSTLING. The unique dedication stone on the north wall of the chancel which records the construction of the church and its dedication on St Eusebius' day.

A few Kent churches have a mausoleum in the churchyard. Although they are mainly confined to nineteenth-century urban cemeteries, three good examples survive in Kent, at Farningham, Boughton Monchelsea and Chiddingstone. The latter is very interesting because it leads directly to a vault, ventilated by a false tomb chest a few feet away with a grating in the side! The mausoleum at Farningham was probably designed by John Nash as it was intended for his uncle, and is built of fine Portland stone.

Sometimes an HOURGLASS STAND may be found next to the pulpit. After the Reformation preaching became much more important, and sermons achieved marathon proportions. To enable the preacher to regulate his output an hourglass was provided, which he could turn over as many times as he thought fit! Both Cliffe and Leigh have examples of the metal stands, minus glass, the latter dated 1597.

Nineteenth-century churches in Kent are well worth a visit. Indeed we have one of the most historically important churches in England at Kilndown. It was constructed by Viscount Beresford in 1841, and over the next few years was beautified by his stepson, Alexander Beresford Hope, one of the founding members of the Camden Society, who believed that Gothic architecture should be structural and not purely decorative, and where possible based on surviving medieval examples.

It became one of the first true Gothic Revival churches to have a full set of 'medieval' furnishings, all of which were a blaze of colour. Despite later alterations it remains one of the highlights of a county that is full of interest.

To see the evolution of decorative Gothic to structural Gothic the reader should visit Ramsgate where the 1827 church of St George stands in marked contrast to Sir George Gilbert Scott's Christ Church of twenty years later.

Where the Victorians added to, or rebuilt parts of, an existing church, their work can be either a blessing or a blight. We usually blame the architect, but it was often intervention from the patron which led to some disastrous alterations. The tower at Leybourne church was rebuilt in the 1870s and adds much to the appearance of the exterior, but one wishes that a more sympathetic local material had been chosen. At Frinsted in 1870 the chancel and chapel were decorated with stencilling on the walls which adds much to the interior. At the same time the exterior walls were tidied up to the extent of creating a 'Victorian church'. At Swingfield a north aisle was added which destroyed the proportions of a simple thirteenth-century building, while at Newenden a spire was added to the remains of a medieval church and demonstrates just how sensitive restorers could be. The same church has a chancel of 1930, again most sympathetically designed. At Erith a north aisle was added and actually incorporated a blocked door and window as if to masquerade as part of the original building! At Cooling a vestry was added to the south side of the church, the interior walls of which are entirely covered with cockle shells in the same style as the Shell Grotto at Margate.

But by far the most drastic restoration of a medieval church was at Wickhambreux. The entire character of the church was altered by the lining of the lower walls with brown glazed tiles. Above the chancel arch are stencilled angels floating up to a blue painted and star-spangled sky! It works surprisingly well, but as in many other churches the Victorian work has not worn at all well, when compared with medieval work.

Map of Kent, showing locations of churches.

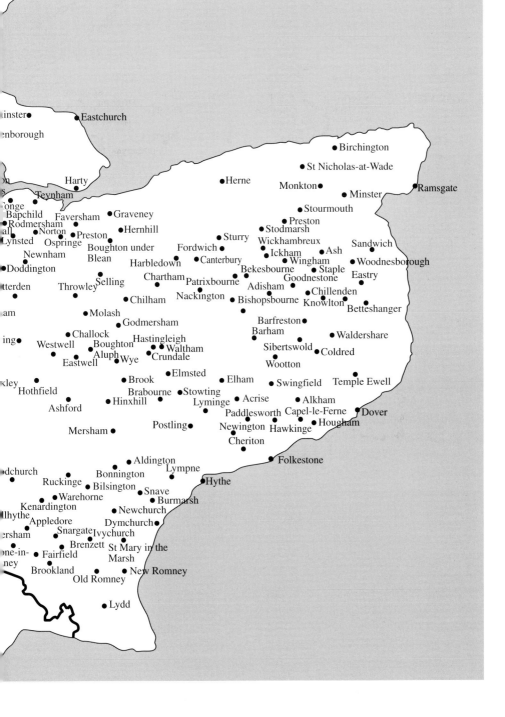

inster● ●Eastchurch

●nborough

●Birchington

●St Nicholas-at-Wade

)n●   Harty   ●Herne   Monkton●
●s   Teynham   ●Minster   ●Ramsgate
onge   ●Stourmouth
●Bapchild Faversham ●Graveney   ●Preston
●Rodmersham   ●Stodmarsh
all● ●Norton ●Preston ●Hernhill   ●Sturry Wickhambreux   Sandwich●
Lynsted Ospringe Boughton under Fordwich●   ●Ickham ●Ash
Newnham   Blean   ●Canterbury ●Wingham   ●Woodnesborough
●Doddington   Harbledown   ●Bekesbourne ●Staple Eastry
                    Chartham ●Patrixbourne   ●Goodnestone
tterden Throwley●Selling   Adisham●   ●Chillenden
                ●Chilham Nackington● ●Bishopsbourne Knowlton● ●Betteshanger
●am   ●Molash   ●Barfreston
            ●Godmersham   Barham●   ●Waldershare
●ing● ●Challock   ●Sibertswold ●Coldred
        Westwell ●Boughton ●Hastingleigh
        ●Eastwell Aluph●Waltham   ●Wootton
                Wye● ●Crundale
●kley   ●Elmsted
    Hothfield ●Brook   ●Elham ●Swingfield Temple Ewell●
                Brabourne●Stowting
Ashford   ●Hinxhill Lyminge● ●Acrise ●Alkham
                                Paddlesworth● Capel-le-Ferne ●Dover
    Mersham●   Postling●   Newington● Hawkinge● Hougham●
                                    ●Cheriton
                        ●Aldington
●dchurch   Bonnington ●Lympne
    ●Ruckinge ●Bilsington   ●Folkestone
            ●Warehorne ●Snave   ●Hythe
    Kenardington   ●Burmarsh
●lhythe ●Appledore ●Newchurch
●rsham   ●Snargate●Ivychurch Dymchurch●
●ne-in- ●Fairfield ●Brenzett St Mary in the
ney   Brookland●   ●Marsh
            Old Romney ●New Romney
                ●Lydd

PART 2

Gazetteer

This section contains brief details of over two hundred Kent churches that offer something of particular interest.

ACRISE, St Matthew

A small, isolated church with many large windows of seventeenth-century date, although the dark Victorian glass does not help illumination. There is hardly any difference between the floor level of nave and chancel, but this goes almost unnoticed as one's eyes are drawn to the extraordinary chancel arch. It is dark, heavily moulded and seems to have been built in the thirteenth century, using older medieval carvings to great effect. To the south is the charming manorial pew, complete with carpet, table dated 1758, and tiny eighteenth-century chairs used by the Sunday School children. The seventeenth-century feel of the nave gives way to a nineteenth-century atmosphere in the chancel, which is dominated by an eight-light brass chandelier in high Victorian style. To either side of the chancel arch are fascinating expanding brass candlesticks which may be swivelled in many directions.

ADDINGTON, St Margaret

This church was built a long way from its village and is entered through a porch with very pretty carved bargeboards. The Norman aisleless nave was extended to the west when the present tower was built in the fifteenth century, and the former outside corner of the Norman building may be clearly seen. The interior was heavily restored in the 1880s, but the south chapel contains much of interest, notably the Watton memorial of 1653 which blocks the former east window, which can be seen outside. The chapel has a nice contemporary painted ceiling.

ADISHAM, *Holy Innocents*

A stately cruciform church that enjoyed wealthy patronage throughout the Middle Ages. In this case it was the monks of Christ Church, Canterbury. Much rebuilding took place in the thirteenth century, typified by the run of lancets in the chancel. The walls show very definite building 'lifts' on the outside, especially notable in the south transept. Inside are several examples of medieval woodwork, including two screens and a reredos brought here in the eighteenth century from Canterbury Cathedral.

ALDINGTON, *St Martin*

A large and impressive church in a farmyard setting. There is some eleventh-century stonework, although the church was much enlarged in the fourteenth and fifteenth centuries under the personal patronage of successive Archbishops of Canterbury. Inside, the base of the rood screen survives, as does a run of fifteen choir stalls. Good quality nineteenth- and twentieth-century stained glass shows the development of the art over the last hundred years and includes the west window by Heaton, Butler and Bayne, and the Risen Christ by Frederick Cole. There is a Norman font with a bulgy cover of seventeenth-century date. In the south wall of the chancel is an elaborate three-seater sedilia, with a blocked doorway as part of the same scheme. The tower dates from the sixteenth century and the stonework clearly shows that it was built as a separate structure and joined to the nave at a later date.

ALKHAM, *St Anthony*

This church displays an excellent example of an early south aisle – a lean-to construction of four bays. There was originally a north aisle also, although this was destroyed when the present north chapel was built in the late thirteenth century. The latter, which is of unusual proportions, has wonderful wall arcading with detached Bethersden marble shafts. On the eastern wall are two brackets to support images and a plain thirteenth-century piscina. The east window of the north chapel consists of a pair of lancets, as opposed to the more usual grouping of three, but their internal shafting more than compensates. There is an aisle clerestory of round windows, while the west window of the north chapel has an enormous circular window, or oculus. The finest monument in the church is a thirteenth-century coffin lid with a very early inscription, translated as, 'Here lieth Herbert, offspring of Simon, a man openhearted, assured by hope of good things, fluent in the word of faith'.

ALLHALLOWS, *All Saints*

A very picturesque church of Norman origin, rebuilt in the late thirteenth and early fourteenth centuries, and again by Christian in 1886. The south aisle battlements lead one's eyes up to the little spirelet. The rood screen, of fourteenth-century date, survives in situ, although it was hardly built on a grand scale. In the chancel is a brass to Thomas Coppinger (d. 1587) which originally stood in a north chapel whose foundations may still be seen. On the opposite side of the chancel stood the vicarage – joined on to the church – but this was demolished in the mid-nineteenth century.

APPLEDORE, *Sts Peter and Paul*

A rather misshapen church entered by a misshapen west tower: the result of French raids of 1380 and later neglect. The whole church was given a sympathetic restoration in 1925 which gave the building much character by removing many of the Victorian additions. There is a fine rood screen which spans both north and south chapels, and an elaborate holy water stoup. The medieval altar slab in the sanctuary still shows its consecration crosses, while nearby there is a good selection of thirteenth-century tiles. Because of its location on the edge of the marshes there are many text boards and a good Royal Arms of George III. Interesting modern stained glass includes a window of Hornes Place which shows an electricity pylon in the bottom left-hand corner! Another recent window has a picture of the church of St Thomas à Becket, Fairfield, surrounded by grazing sheep.

ASH, *St Nicholas*

A large and impressive church of mainly thirteenth-century date, over-restored in 1847 by the irrepressible William Butterfield. The scale of the interior is impressive – particularly in the tower arches which support the tall needle spire. They date from the Perpendicular period and are an obvious insertion into the original structure. The best furnishing at Ash is the charming marble font which dates from 1726. It has a wide shallow octagonal bowl on an inscribed base. For the visitor interested in memorials, Ash has more to offer than most, ranging from the fourteenth-century effigy of a knight under an unfortunately damaged canopy to two excellent alabaster hanging memorials to Sir Thomas Harfleet (d. 1612) and Christopher Toldervy (d. 1618). Mrs Toldervy appears twice in the church for she accompanies her husband kneeling at a prie-dieu on his monument, and again as a weeping figure on the base of her parents' memorial! On that structure she is one of two surviving daughters in a total of seven. Her weeping brothers have all disappeared over the course of time.

ASH NEXT WROTHAM, Sts Peter and Paul

As you walk up the path the eighteenth-century brick repair of the west tower blends very well with the medieval flint rubble construction. A large and well-lit church with an excellent crownpost roof. The two windows over the chancel arch originally threw light on to the rood figures. To the north of the chancel is the Lady Chapel with small fragments of medieval glass in the window tracery. For most of the eighteenth and nineteenth centuries this was used as the Hodsall family chapel and there is a fine series of ledger stones commemorating them. In the chancel an alabaster hanging monument to the Maxfields (d. 1605) is rather fun, with their grumpy kneeling figures facing each other. All the main furnishings date from the twentieth century and were designed by Sir T.G. Jackson in a traditional style sympathetic to the character of the building.

ASHFORD, St Mary

Seen from afar, the tower looks unusually slim – not helped by its uncharacteristic pinnacles that date from the fifteenth century. The church contains some interesting monuments and fittings, the majority of which are found in the south transept, commemorating members of the Smythe family who were prominent in the town in the sixteenth and seventeenth centuries. The Royal Arms of carved and painted wood are dated 1660 and are a rare and early example of arms of Charles II. Early memorial brass to the Countess of Atholl (d. 1375), and stained glass by Lavers and Barraud, Willement and Kempe add to the interest of the interior. The stone pulpit of 1897 is by John Loughborough Pearson, and the oak chancel screen of 1920 by W.D. Caroe. In the chancel is a series of medieval misericords.

AYLESFORD, Sts Peter and Paul

The position of the church, high above the village square, shows its important strategic location. The base of the tower dates from the Norman period, but the rest of the church is the result of fourteenth- and fifteenth-century rebuilds. Heavily restored in the nineteenth century, the church luckily keeps many original features, including the rood loft stairway, the corbels that supported the

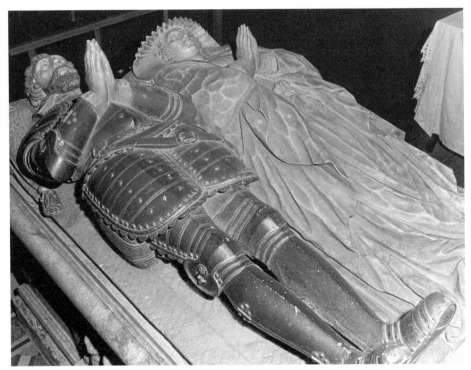

AYLESFORD. Sir Thomas Colepepper and wife. An early seventeenth-century alabaster tomb chest which retains its original paint.

rood beam and a hagioscope at the west end. There is an impressive alabaster monument to Sir Thomas Colepepper (d. 1605) and a towering marble structure to Sir John Banks (d. 1699). The latter is probably by John Nost, court sculptor to William and Mary whose elaborate Royal Arms of carved and gilded wood hang over the vestry door. Nearby is an oil painting showing the former almshouse chapel in the early 1900s. There is a collection of mediocre Victorian glass, punctuated by two windows by the firm of Clayton and Bell. The font was carved by John Thomas, the famous nineteenth-century sculptor who worked at Windsor Castle and the Palace of Westminster.

BARFRESTONE, St Nicholas

Barfrestone is arguably the most famous church in Kent. It dates entirely from the late twelfth century and consists of a two-cell structure built of imported Caen limestone. It stands on a slope overlooking a charming valley

BARFRESTONE. Tall and impressive twelfth-century chancel arch with rere-arches to north and south that would have served side altars.

and seems to 'belong' to the countryside. The exterior is elaborately carved with heads and grotesques. By far the most outstanding feature is the south doorway which depicts Our Lord in Glory. Around the arch are wonderful – albeit weathered – medallions of the signs of the zodiac and the labours of the month. The smooth jambs of the doorway have the remains of several mass dials, while the north doorway has some elaborate medieval graffiti. Inside, the church has a frieze with many human and animal figures, although on closer inspection it is obvious that much of what is visible is the result of nineteenth-century restorations.

BARHAM, St John the Baptist

A long and light church, best appreciated from the south. Like Ickham it is cruciform in plan, with a west tower rather than one in the more usual position over the crossing. This is not a case of a tower being added to an earlier building, as the tower is of undoubted twelfth- or early thirteenth-century stonework. Lord Kitchener's name appears on the war memorial, as he lived in the parish. At the west end of the south aisle is the elaborate monument of Sir Basil Dixwell (d. 1750). One only wishes it stood in a position where it could be better appreciated. There is some poor quality nineteenth-century glass, and two twentieth-century windows by Martin Travers. That in the main east window, of 1925, shows Our Lady and Child beneath a typical Travers detail – a baroque canopy. Under the tower, affixed to the wall, are some Flanders tiles purchased in the will of John Digge who died in 1375. His memorial brass survives in the vestry.

BARMING, St Margaret

An isolated church at the end of a lane above the River Medway. Norman origins are obvious – three windows in the east wall indicate the earliest work. The nave is also early, and to this was added a fifteenth-century tower with stair turret and needle-like spire. The north aisle is a nineteenth-century addition, and the chancel was restored by Comper. It represents some of his earliest work, although much of its impact has been lost by subsequent modification. The outstanding feature of the church is the set of wooden carvings that seem to have originated in the Rhine valley. They are of early fourteenth-century date and show enormous figures of St Michael, Our Lord and Samson. Although they form bench ends they stand high above the benches and dominate the chancel in an almost alarming manner!

BEKESBOURNE, *St Peter*

A pretty church which suffered badly at the hands of the nineteenth-century restorer when the nave walls were stripped of plaster and the west tower rebuilt. The Norman north doorway is of considerable size – for the Archbishops of Canterbury had a palace here in the Middle Ages, and their wealth is shown in the structure. The thirteenth-century string course in the chancel emphasizes the changes in floor level, and there are two aumbries in the east wall behind the altar. There is a rather stilted kneeling figure of Sir Henry Palmer (d. 1611) at a prayer desk under an Ionic portal, carved in marble with two small Bethersden marble insets under the arch. Another large marble monument commemorates Sir Thomas Pym Hales Bt (d. 1773), who is described as having 'increasing Benevolence to Mankind'. There is some poor thirteenth-century glass and a contemporary double piscina.

BETTESHANGER, *St Mary*

One of the most attractive Victorian churches in Kent, paid for by Sir Walter James in 1853, in imitation of nearby Barfrestone. The architect was Anthony Salvin, who effectively rebuilt an existing church. A few objects remain from the earlier building including a thirteenth-century piscina, the Royal Arms of William III and a memorial with a naval theme to Salmon Morris designed by Peter Scheemakers. A large and imposing Byzantine porch protects the tympanum over the south door and leads the visitor to an elaborate and rich interior of great character. Good quality Victorian fittings range from the pulpit and reredos to stained glass by Kempe.

BEXLEY, *St Mary*

There is a surprisingly rural feel to the setting of Bexley church – even though it is surrounded by twentieth-century development. The west tower is surmounted by a spire whose shape changes midway up, from pyramidal to octagonal. The whole church is most attractive. Some mass dials may be seen on the south side of the chancel. Inside, the remains of a Norman arch over the south doorway indicate the early origins of this otherwise thirteenth- to fifteenth-century church. Good quality late nineteenth-century woodwork of screen, stalls and pulpit, and lots of hanging monuments show that money was abundant in the Victorian era. The earliest monument is that to Sir John Champneis who lived at Hall Place in the late sixteenth century. The architect who restored the church in the nineteenth century was Basil Champneys who claimed to be a descendant. A recent addition to the excellent furnishings is the window of a globe and sundial designed by Nicola Kantorowicz in 1991.

BIDBOROUGH, St Lawrence

Bidborough church stands on a steep knoll overlooking a marvellously green valley. The south doorway is Norman, although it was moved and rebuilt when the church was enlarged in the nineteenth century. The chancel is tastefully furnished – light wooden panelling surrounds the walls and a blue carpet complements the stained glass windows that are mostly by Burne-Jones for Morris and Co. By far the most memorable feature of the interior is the swinging pendulum of the clock which hangs below the west window of the tower. It is suitably inscribed, but one only wishes that it would stop so that the inscription could be read with ease!

BIDDENDEN, All Saints

Set at the end of the High Street, the asymmetry of the building is most pleasing. The church is basically thirteenth century in its fabric which was much altered in the fourteenth century when the present crownpost roof of the nave was built. This is the area of Kent that produced Bethersden marble, so it is not surprising to see this material used to great effect in the font, sedilia and piscina. A good selection of memorial brasses includes one to Margaret Godwell who died in 1499. The last line of its inscription has been obliterated – a common occurrence in the late sixteenth century when prayers for the souls of the dead were no longer considered appropriate.

BILSINGTON, Sts Peter and Paul

Originally a Norman church (there is a blocked window over the south door) but enlarged by an extension of the chancel in the thirteenth century, and the addition of a short tower in the fifteenth. The latter was never completed and is surmounted by a timber-shingled belfry. The chancel arch is plainest thirteenth-century work, and frames the east window of three lancets. These are, in fact, Victorian replacements. Although they are probably shorter than the thirteenth century would have produced, their exterior appearance – with no hood moulds – is quite convincing. There are some fine early nineteenth-century text boards and an exceptional Royal Arms of 1774, with two tiny bewigged heads on the plinth. The twentieth-century reredos in the style of Comper is by Kruger Gay.

BIRCHINGTON, All Saints

All Saints is a large church in a prominent position in the centre of Birchington. Like most churches in this part of Kent it dates from the thirteenth and fourteenth centuries, but was extensively rebuilt in 1864. It is the furnishing and not the building that the visitor will remember. The font is a charming piece of thirteenth-century workmanship with the octagonal bowl sitting on a large drum of stone, supported by four slender pillars – one at each corner. It still shows the mark of its former lock. In the Quex Chapel are some splendid monuments of the sixteenth to eighteenth centuries, the finest of which is the 'six bust monument' to celebrate several members of the Crispe family. The reredos to the main altar was painted by N.H.J. Westlake and depicts the Last Supper, surrounded by local seventh-century saints. Westlake also designed the east and west windows. Another famous artist, F.J. Shields, designed an impressive window which commemorates Dante Gabriel Rossetti, who is buried in the churchyard under a cross designed by another member of the Pre-Raphaelite Brotherhood, Ford Madox Brown.

BIRLING, All Saints

Birling is an estate village which owes its character to the Nevill family, who have been associated with the area since at least the fifteenth century. The church also mirrors their patronage and contains much of interest. All Saints is an airy church which stands on a mound overlooking the centre of the village, the main feature of its exterior being the very narrow tower with an oversized stair turret. The church dates in the main from the fourteenth and fifteenth centuries, although the furnishings, which give the building so much character, date from the nineteenth century. The enormous font cover was carved by three sisters of the Nevill family in 1853 and their initials may still be seen pencilled on the inner faces of the inset panels. In the centre of the chancel floor, in front of the altar rails, is the cast-iron door to the Nevill family vault. It is easily identified by their crest – the Nevill bull. There are many other reminders of the family including hatchments, shields and plaques.

BISHOPSBOURNE, St Mary

A mainly thirteenth-century church restored by Scott. There is a high window which originally shed light on the rood figures. Some medieval glass survives in the heads of the windows in the chancel showing angels carrying crowns. In the west window is an 1874 design by Morris and Co. to commemorate a former rector. The north chapel has a stone shelf that once served as a retable for an altar, while the south chapel has a collection of continental glass panels brought here by the Beckingham family from their home in Essex. There are some fairly good murals above the nave arcade – including a figure of St Nicholas – and plenty of characteristic thirteenth-century red-painted masonry joints. In the chancel the memorial to Richard Hooker, the famous Elizabethan theologian, attracts much attention.

BOBBING, St Bartholomew

Recently restored, the church displays far more of interest than the exterior promises. The church dates from the early years of the fourteenth century and consists of nave, chancel, north aisle and tower. The south chancel wall contains an outstanding square-headed low side window which contains its original medieval ironwork. Next to it is a nice sedilia which includes a piece of twelfth-century carving in Caen stone. It was probably brought here as rubble from Canterbury Cathedral during its rebuilding and depicts two figures – a bishop and a priest. The bishop is identified at St Martial, the first Bishop of Limoges, and shows great artistic quality for so early a date. His robes fall in front of him so as to form an 'eye' pattern and his hirsute appearance shows a face full of character. There are also two fine fifteenth-century brasses to Sir Arnold and Lady Savage. On the outside of the porch are the remains of two mass dials. A late seventeenth-century vicar of Bobbing was Titus Oates, who plotted against Catholic supporters and so gained a place in national history.

BONNINGTON, St Rumwold

Rumwold was a seventh-century saint about whom very little is known. There are only eight churches dedicated to him. Bonnington is a small two-cell church of great charm which stands on the banks of the Royal Military Canal. The building is of fourteenth-century appearance which resulted from a major reconstruction of a Saxo-Norman original. The east wall contains three Norman windows. There is no difference between floor level in nave and chancel, which creates a homely and less mysterious feel. Next to the chancel arch is a small image niche, above which is a bracket which would have supported the rood beam. On the south side is an enormous pulpit with a large sounding board, while over the chancel arch is a large Royal Arms of George III dated 1774. The north-west window contains fragments of medieval glass, including three little heads.

BORDEN, *Sts Peter and Paul*

A wonderful Norman tower shows the typical proportions of the period. It is set off well by a good rood loft staircase at the south junction of nave and chancel. Good twelfth-century west door and Norman arch from tower to nave. The chancel was later extended north and south by the addition of the chapels, with the original quoins being clearly visible on the outside of the east wall. The church was heavily restored in the nineteenth century – but its two outstanding features survive. One, a fifteenth-century wall painting of St Christopher opposite the south door, is typically found in churches on main routes of travel. The other feature, a monument to Robert Plot (d. 1671), father of the well-known seventeenth-century historian, is the finest memorial of its date in Kent and shows St Michael slaying the Devil.

BOUGHTON ALUPH, *All Saints*

This large thirteenth-century church was extensively rebuilt a hundred years later. The lord of the manor in the fourteenth century was Thomas de Aldon, yeoman to Edward III, and it was probably he who paid for the rebuilding, as several of his fellow courtiers are represented by stained glass coats of arms in the windows. The east window figures, under a scene of the Coronation of the Virgin, are traditionally those of Edward III and Queen Philippa of Hainault. The tracery of the window itself consists of a 'ladder' of eight Perpendicular panels over five large lights of equal height. Many other windows were reduced in size in the nineteenth century when their outer lights were bricked in to reduce the area of glass. The brick porch contains a lovely little fireplace and may have been constructed with the comfort of the traveller in mind.

BOUGHTON MALHERBE, *St Nicholas*

This church deserves to be better known and has one of the most scholarly guidebooks of any in the county. Like most of the churches in the area it dates in the main from the fourteenth century, but was much restored in the nineteenth by a local builder who obviously had knowledge of the work of the Camden Society, at that time promoting correct 'ecclesiological' restorations. The most amazing aspect of the church is the huge difference in floor level between nave and chancel. While this more than satisfies the nineteenth-century requirements it may be an older feature, as Sir Stephen Glynne recorded a 'considerable ascent to the chancel' before the restoration. There are some interesting memorials to the Wotton family who lived nearby. A nice marble bust commemorates Thomas Wotton (d. 1587) while three marble lions survive from a memorial of 1664, the main part of which now floors the vestry! The pulpit is Elizabethan, but most of the stalls and interesting wooden screens are mid-nineteenth century. Good stained glass includes the west window (Kempe, 1894) and east window (Warrington, 1850).

BOUGHTON MONCHELSEA, St Peter

A church whose interior does not quite deliver all its picturesque exterior promises. The situation on the end of the sandstone ridge with far-ranging views is wonderful – and the lychgate is one of the oldest in the county, probably dating from the fifteenth century. Inside, the results of a serious fire in 1832 and subsequent rebuildings are all too obvious. The plaster has been stripped from the walls and the rubble stonework disastrously repointed, while the poor quality mid-nineteenth-century glass installed by Hardman's studio is not typical of their usual high quality output. However, the stone and alabaster reredos is just the right scale for the chancel, and blends in nicely with the medieval aumbry, piscina and sedilia. There is also a good range of eighteenth- and nineteenth-century memorials including a large piece at the west end by Scheemakers to Sir Christopher Powell (d. 1742).

BOUGHTON UNDER BLEAN, Sts Peter and Paul

A large church which shows nothing earlier than the thirteenth century. The sixteenth-century rood screen has a Victorian loft, and the medieval staircase that gave access to it survives in the north aisle. The north chapel contains an excellent monument to Sir Thomas Hawkins (d. 1617), signed by Epiphanius Evesham, and just slightly earlier than his work at Lynsted (see separate entry). There is in addition a fine crownpost roof in the nave, parclose screens to north and south chapels and a small thirteenth-century piscina.

BOXLEY, St Mary and All Saints

The church lies at the far end of the village green. Visitors who do not first walk around the church wonder if they are ever going to get in – for they have to walk through two rooms first! From the outside it is not so puzzling; the first room is in fact the nave of the Norman church. Then comes the base of the fifteenth-century tower, built on the site of the Norman chancel. Only after we have gone through this do we come to the church proper – a complete fourteenth-century structure. It is wide, with two aisles, and relatively short. The chancel is well proportioned and has a definite lean to the south.

BRABOURNE, St Mary

St Mary's is a very tall church, more Saxon in its proportions than Norman. The church dates in its present form from the twelfth century, with typical decoration in the form of pilaster buttresses on the outside north wall of the chancel. In the thirteenth century a south aisle was added and the present arch to the tower rebuilt; the remains of the original Norman arch may still be seen. In the chancel is a remarkable survivor – a twelfth-century window with its original glass. It has been reset and restored, but vividly recalls the dusky colours of the period. The pattern is purely geometric, of flowers and semi-circles, and may be compared to the contemporary glass of Canterbury Cathedral. Also in the chancel is one of the two thirteenth-century heart shrines in Kent. This little piece of sculpture consists of a plain shield – originally painted – under decorated and cusped tracery, the whole squeezed between thin pinnacles. It is uncertain whose heart was buried here, but it dates from about 1296 and may be associated with the de Valence family. The other Kent heart shrine is at Leybourne (see separate entry).

BREDGAR, St John the Baptist

This is a collegiate church, with much work of the fourteenth and fifteenth centuries. When the college was founded by Robert de Bredgar in 1393 the nave and south aisle were completely rebuilt. It was a case of premature enlargement, for the college was a very small foundation and seems to have used the existing north chapel for its services. In all events, the very cheap form of sedilia in the chancel – a dropped window-sill – shows that very little money was left after the completion of the west tower. This meant that there was insufficient cash for the west door and instead of introducing a brand new feature, they re-used a Norman doorway! This reinforces the point that one should never date a wall by the architectural features within it. There is a small brass of one of the collegiate priests, Thomas Coly (d. 1518), while the house in which he lived survives on the opposite side of the road.

BRENCHLEY, All Saints

All Saints is an interesting church standing in a beautifully kept churchyard. The crownpost roof incorporates a canopy of honour over the eastern bay, where it would have emphasized the position of the rood. The lower part of the rood screen survives and is dated 1536 – making it (with Lullingstone) one of the last to be built in Kent before the Reformation. The sedilia and piscina survive in the chancel and date from the fourteenth century, even though this part of the church was rebuilt in the nineteenth century. The east window is by Morris and Co., and dates from 1910, while the windows to north and south of the sanctuary are also twentieth century and are by Robert Anning Bell. There is a fine memorial in the north transept to Barbara and Walter Roberts, showing the two figures holding hands. It dates from 1652. One of the bells in the tower carries the inscription, 'Untouched I am a silent thing, But strike me and I sweetly sing.'

BRENZETT, St Eanswyth

One of the few churches in the county dedicated to a local saint: St Eanswyth came from Folkestone (see separate entry). The church is Norman with thirteenth- and fourteenth-century additions. The south wall of the chancel contains some of the fine herringbone masonry so typical of early Norman work in Kent. Like most churches on Romney Marsh there is an abundance of clear glass at Brenzett, allowing a greater appreciation of the superb tracery of the decorated style windows, especially that in the south nave wall. When the little spire was built in the fourteenth century a wooden frame had to be erected at the west end to support it, and enormous buttresses had to be built outside. The church was over-restored in the nineteenth century when the east window by Lavers, Barraud and Westlake was installed. The north chapel contains a good monument in alabaster to Sir John Fagge who died in 1639. Father and son lie side by side, one propped on his elbow, the other with his hand on his chest. Their armorial bearings on the front of the tomb chest add a welcome splash of red and white.

BROOK, St Mary

Since its re-ordering in 1986 Brook church has shown the visitor what a church interior might have looked like in the twelfth century. The chancel is empty except for the stone altar, discovered a few years ago in the churchyard, and now set on two ragstone pillars. The church is large, for throughout the medieval period it belonged to Christ Church, Canterbury. There is much Norman work to be seen, including the three-stage west tower which contains a purpose-built chapel or westwerk. The church has a comprehensive series of thirteenth-century wall paintings, overlain by some fourteenth- and seventeenth-century murals, although the early paintings are not as well preserved as they could be. In the north wall of the chancel is a small almond-shaped hagioscope to the exterior. It may have connected to an anchorite's cell, but is more likely to have been associated with the exposition of a relic on the high altar. It is certainly not a low side window as the tower bell would have been used for this purpose.

BROOKLAND, St Augustine

A long low church with the most famous spire in Kent. This three-stage 'candle-snuffer' erection is the result of several enlargements of a thirteenth-century bell cage and its subsequent weatherproofing with cedar shingles. It contains a peal of six bells, the oldest of which is mid-fifteenth century in date. The spire is surmounted by a winged dragon weathervane, dating from 1797. The monster has a prominent forked tongue. The reason for the bells being hung in a cage rather than a tower is shown inside the church where the pillars of the nave have sunk into the soft ground and splayed out to north and south. The tie-beams of the roof came away from the walls and have had to be lengthened by the addition of new timber supports. The outstanding Norman font in cast lead has been fully described in Part 1.

BROOKLAND. The famous medieval spire which stands on the ground to the north of the church. It was built in that form to allow for settlement in the marshy ground.

BURHAM, St Mary

The church was abandoned in 1881 when a new church (since demolished) was built in a more convenient position on the hill above. There was a medieval ferry across the river here and Burham church displays much similarity with that of Snodland on the opposite bank. Norman work is prominent – including two twelfth-century windows (one blocked) and the use of tufa blocks as part of the rubble construction. In the thirteenth century aisles were built, and although they were subsequently demolished, the blocked arches remain, as does part of the rood loft staircase. The three-stage tower dates from the fifteenth century and has a SW stair turret which gives good views across the Medway Valley. Burham church was rescued from dereliction in the 1950s by the Friends of Friendless Churches and is now lovingly cared for by the Churches Conservation Trust.

BURMARSH, All Saints

The south doorway is Burmarsh's claim to fame. It is good late twelfth-century carving with a roll moulded arch surmounted by triple chevrons and billets. In the centre of the billets is a large carved human head – of a man who, from his expression, is suffering from toothache! The doorway is in its original position, although in Tudor times a new smaller doorway was inserted within the same frame, just below the capitals of the original. Another Norman feature to be seen is the window in the north chancel wall, its head cut from a single piece of stone. There is a pretty twentieth-century chancel screen and paintings on the chancel ceiling done by a former rector. The Royal Arms are those of George III and are signed as the work of J. Marten whose work may also be seen at Staplehurst and Hinxhill. Two mass dials survive on the SW buttress of the tower which dates from the fourteenth century.

CANTERBURY, St Dunstan

Dedicated to a former Archbishop of Canterbury, St Dunstan's stands outside the city walls. There is structural evidence of the Norman period, but most of the church is fourteenth century. The west tower dates from this time and is very oddly proportioned – about twice the height that its width can really cope with. The south chapel is constructed of brickwork and was completed in the early sixteenth century. It contains monuments to the More family and is the burial place of Thomas More's head – brought here by his daughter after his execution. The family home stood opposite the church. There are two twentieth-century windows of note in the chapel, by Lawrence Lee and John Hayward.

CANTERBURY, St Martin

Historically, this is the most important church in Kent. St Martin's is the building in which Queen Bertha and St Augustine worshipped together in the closing years of the sixth century, making it the oldest parish church in England that is still in use. Furthermore it is built of large quantities of Roman tile mixed with local flint and ragstone. The exterior shows typical Saxon buttresses and long and short work, but there are no Saxon window openings still in use. However, the west wall inside has been stripped of plaster which allows us to see very early blocked windows. Apart from the great age of the walls there is little of visual interest – with a fourteenth-century tower at the west end and a rather severe atmosphere resulting from the drastic nineteenth-century restoration that saw the insertion of dreadful 'catalogue' stained glass. Were it not for the early history of this church the font would be its outstanding feature. It is of Norman date and is carved from a large block of Caen stone. Tall, solid, and eminently decorative it has intersecting circlets in two lower levels, and arcading of Romanesque arches above, topped by a rim of rolling swags. In the churchyard is the grave of Mary Tourtel, creator of Rupert Bear.

CAPEL, St Thomas Becket

A Norman church, much rebuilt in the seventeenth century following a storm, and again in the early twentieth century. A twelfth-century window survives in the north wall of the nave, but most of the windows are later. The altar rails are dated 1682 and are good examples of the period. The Royal Arms of George II are dated 1739. Most people remember this church for its wall paintings which were rediscovered – whitewashed over – in 1927. These are dated to the mid-thirteenth century and were painted in two tiers along the north nave wall. If the south wall had not been rebuilt in the later Middle Ages that too might have yielded further murals. Those that survive cover a variety of scenes including a good Entry into Jerusalem, Cain and Abel and the Last Supper. The paintings were restored by Professor Tristram, but luckily he concentrated on conservation and repainted very little. There are also some later murals to either side of the chancel arch. The church is now cared for by the Churches Conservation Trust.

CAPEL LE FERNE, St Mary

The parish derives its name from the 'church among the ferns', although today this windswept building shelters few plants other than hardy grass. The church is of flint and rubble construction and is not graceful. The west tower is mean and the stone dressings do not blend well with the main rubble walls. However, the dressings on the north-east corner of the chancel do show some interesting graffiti – DV1739. One enters the church from the south via a very large porch which shelters a tiny arched doorway opening into the centre of the nave. To the left all is plain, but to the right is the most memorable chancel screen in the county. It is built of stone and consists of three arches. Above is a large arch which would have contained the rood figures, and the corbels to support the rood beam are still to be seen. In addition there is a tiny window high in the north wall of the nave to shed extra light on to the figures. Next to it is the only surviving Norman window and a lovely picture in twentieth-century glass. The Norman splays still show their original painted decoration, very similar to that at Leybourne. In complete contrast to the narrow south door the arch to the tower is wide and worthy of note. The floor is entirely covered with Victorian tiles, although several ledger slabs do survive. The font is unusual in that it is of great bulk, with a minute receptacle for the holy water in the middle of it! The church is well cared for by the Churches Conservation Trust, much supported by a number of local residents.

CHALK, St Mary the Virgin

A rather incongruous porch slaps up to the fifteenth-century west tower that acts as a landmark on the former A2 London–Dover road. The church is Norman in origin, but much rebuilt. In the twelfth century a north aisle was added and the arcade from the nave shows the pointed arches simply cut through the existing wall. A hundred years later a south aisle was built, but this was demolished in 1759. The circular pillars, as opposed to the rectangular piers opposite, may be clearly seen and add much to the character of the church. The east window is a group of three lancets, although they are much restored. In the south wall of the chancel is a good example of a thirteenth-century low side window, while in the north chapel are two tomb recesses of fourteenth-century date. Charles Dickens worshipped in this church and would raise his hat to the jolly monk whose carving may still be seen over the west doorway!

CHALK. The arcade to the south aisle which was constructed in the thirteenth century and demolished in 1759.

CHALLOCK, *Sts Cosmas and Damian*

One of the most isolated churches in Kent, situated on a lane that was closed to through traffic following the emparkation of Eastwell in the sixteenth century. The church is built of flint rubble and displays an interesting inset flint cross on the west face of the tower. There is little stained glass as the church was severely damaged in the Second World War, but it is a direct result of that damage that has produced the wall paintings for which the church is famous. When it was rebuilt two art students painted a series of murals in the north chapel to show stories from the lives of the patron saints, Cosmas and Damian. The figures are dumpy and stylized and altogether great fun! At the same time the chancel walls were painted by John Ward RA with scenes from the life of Christ. These are more naturalistic and include portraits of local people in modern costume. One other furnishing of note survives – a prickett beam in the north chapel which was built in the fourteenth century to take votive candles, and a veil to hide the altar from view during Lent.

CHARING, Sts Peter and Paul

A large church beautifully positioned next to the medieval remains of the Archbishop's Palace just off the High Street. The west tower was built in the late fifteenth century. During its construction the body of the church was destroyed in an accidental fire – started by a man shooting at pigeons on the roof. The replacement roofs are clearly dated on the tie-beams as 1592 and 1620. A fine early seventeenth-century pulpit and nice collection of eighteenth-century tablets add much to the character of the building. The south nave window is a very strange shape, basically square, with four lights of equal height surmounted by a net of elaborate triangles, quatrefoils and, unusually, an octofoil! It is of fourteenth-century date.

CHARTHAM, St Mary

There are few churches in Kent that display transepts without a central tower. When in the fifteenth century a tower *was* built it was added to the west end of the existing nave. Two excellent hagioscopes are cut through either side of the chancel arch, while the south transept contains some eighteenth-century monuments by Michael Rysbrack. The most famous memorial at Chartham is the brass to Sir Robert de Septvans (d. 1306), one of the oldest and largest memorial brasses in the country, showing the cross-legged knight with flowing locks. The chancel windows show excellent medieval tracery which has preserved much of its late thirteenth-century glass.

CHERITON, St Martin

A little-known and rarely visited church of Saxon origin. A double splayed window gives it away, and it is thought that the base of the thirteenth-century tower may have been a Saxon porch. The outstanding feature of Cheriton is the decorative arcading in the chancel. It consists of six deeply set arches to north and south. The shafts are of local Bethersden marble and are very finely carved. The lancet windows above are not placed centrally over the arcading – an unusual variation. A further oddity is the fact that the arcading does not include sedilia, which were almost a prerequisite of thirteenth-century rebuilding. Yet there is a sedilia in the south aisle, which dates from a hundred years later. Near the sedilia is a rustic standing monument of a woman.

CHEVENING, St Botolph

The memory which most visitors will take away with them is one of white walls, blue carpet and blocked arches. The nave is exceptionally long but, surprisingly, the south aisle is shorter, leaving one bay of the nave and tower base almost as an appendage at the west end. Along the north and south walls are blocked arches – those in the south aisle obviously tomb recesses, and one still contains a thirteenth-century coffin lid. In the north wall the arches are more interesting. It is possible that they did not lead to a north aisle and were erected as a form of wall decoration. The south chapel contains a series of monuments to the Lennards and Stanhopes who lived in neighbouring Chevening House. One peers through the glazed screens to appreciate how many generations of worthies are buried there – represented by a series of monuments, sculptures, hatchments and heraldry. There is some fine modern stained glass by Moira Forsyth and Keith and Judy Hill.

CHIDDINGSTONE, St Mary

St Mary's church is built of local sandstone, although it is not quite as mellow as neighbouring Leigh and Penshurst. In the churchyard is a fine mausoleum built in 1736 by Henry Streatfield leading down into a large vault ingeniously ventilated by a current of air that enters from the side of a false altar tomb nearby. Inside, the church is almost rectangular, emphasized by the wooden panelling and benches which run round the walls in a most unusual fashion. It was common in the Middle Ages to have stone benches along the walls for the elderly and infirm, but these wooden seats are of much later late. The internal walls of the nave are not rendered, which tends to darken the building, but at the east end of the church, in the north chapel, are some very fine masons' marks. Also in this chapel is a five-light window containing two lights of stained glass dated 1871. It was intended to portray the Last Supper but money must have run out before it was even half-finished!

CHILHAM, St Mary

This large sombre church stands just off the picturesque village square. Dating mainly from the fifteenth century, its interior was much restored in the Victorian period. The visitor today should spend time studying the stained glass and monuments which all commemorate the families associated with the village. In the north aisle is an excellent polished memorial to Sir Dudley

Digges who lived in Chilham Castle in the early seventeenth century. It is made of Bethersden marble, and is similar in workmanship to many fireplaces in the castle. In the north chapel is a memorial to the Hardy children who died in 1858. It shows them reading a book with their toys around them. Originally made for the castle it was presented to the church in 1919. The fine examples of stained glass in the north and south windows are also memorials to the Hardy family, designed by Kempe and Tower in 1914.

CHILLENDEN, All Saints

Standing high on a slope above the valley floor, this two-cell church is of Norman origin and was sensitively restored by Scott in 1871. Both north and south doorways are of the twelfth century – the former being protected by one of Scott's typical openwork porches. The south door has some excellent medieval graffiti of interlacing patterns. One of the best features inside is the tall pulpit of seventeenth-century date which stands next to an excellent wooden chancel screen by Scott. It shows how much character could be introduced by a good nineteenth-century restoration. The chancel roof is rather fun – painted with lively crowns and stars!

CHILLENDEN. The small seventeenth-century pulpit with a sounding board is in the style of a half-tester bed canopy. The screen to the left of this view is by Scott and dates from 1871.

CHISLEHURST, St Nicholas

In the Middle Ages Chislehurst was a small village whose manor house – Scadbury – was home to the powerful Walsingham family. Their influence and that of their followers may be found throughout this charming church. Sir Edward Walsingham's tomb chest (1549) dominates the Scadbury chapel on the north side of the nave. Nearby is an excellent mural monument to Lord Thomas Bertie (d. 1749) designed by Cheere which shows a naval battle in full swing. The village became prosperous in the nineteenth century, and as a result the church contains much work of this period. The ornate reredos was designed by Bodley in 1896. There are several windows by Kempe and his firm, together with some good quality postwar glass to replace that damaged by bombs. In the large and well-kept churchyard is the grave of a local builder, William Willett (1856–1915), who proposed 'daylight saving' or English Summer Time.

CLIFFE, St Helen

An absolute knockout of a church. From the first glimpse of the exterior, with its zebra-like stripes of flint and stone, you know that here is a church of great interest. In plan it consists of an aisled nave, transepts, chancel and west tower – all built on a prodigious scale. Although the church was heavily restored on two occasions in the nineteenth century there is still a great deal of interest. The pillars of the nave have distinctive 'V' paintings contemporary with their fourteenth-century construction. The pulpit is of 1636 and shows some excellent carved arcading. Attached to it is a wrought-iron hourglass stand. The north transept has wall paintings depicting the martyrdom of St Edmund, but these were over-touched-up by Professor Tristram in 1932. Further paintings exist in the south transept and probably show the martyrdom of St Margaret. The base of the rood screen is fifteenth century while the rather insubstantial traceried top is an early twentieth-century addition. There is an elaborate tie-beam high in the roof with little quatrefoil piercings in the spandrels, but this did not support a rood as the remains of the rood loft staircase may be seen in its usual position. Outside the north chancel wall can be found a piscina and holy water stoup – all that remains of a medieval chantry chapel which has been demolished. The blocked-up doorway that originally gave access to it may be seen both inside and out. On the inside south wall of the chancel is one of the finest sedilia in Kent which together with its double piscina dates from the early years of the fourteenth century.

COBHAM, St Mary Magdalene

In a county with more memorial brasses than any other, Cobham takes pride of place, with a set of nineteen, the majority of which are grouped together in the chancel. The church consists of a thirteenth-century chancel, and fourteenth-century nave, aisles and west tower. In 1362 the church was refounded as a college by Sir John de Cobham, and the medieval domestic buildings survive to the south of the church. The south wall of the chancel displays several items of interest. There is a fine double piscina which has been moved further west of its original position. The latter is now occupied by an elaborate fourteenth-century piscina, with a finely wrought canopy of three arches and a parapet of quatrefoils and leaves. Next to it is a slightly plainer sedilia of three equal arches. The last feature of note is the stairway in the south-east corner of the chancel which led to a gallery over the altar – a unique feature in Kent. In the centre of the chancel is the alabaster table tomb of Sir George Brooke (d. 1558). It was badly damaged when a beam fell on it in the eighteenth century and is much restored. In front of the monument are sixteen of the medieval brasses, the most interesting of which are: Sir John de Cobham (d. 1407), founder of the college, who is seen holding a lovely spired church in his hands; Sir Nicholas Hawkberk (d. 1407) – a super visor hinges from his face; William Tanner (d. 1418) the first master of the collegiate foundation.

COLDRED, St Pancras

A sweet little church set in a well-kept churchyard which occupies part of an early bank and ditch fortification. It consists of a two-cell building, quite possibly of Saxon date, as the quoins are not of dressed Norman stonework. The surviving windows in the north and west walls are Norman in appearance and there is a rather nice blocked circular window visible on the outside of the west wall. The interior is simple and unassuming with few memorials – a good ledger slab in the floor of the chancel commemorates Mary Ockman, while a simple marble tablet records the death of 25-year-old Charley Fox on HMS *Vanguard* in June 1917. The great historical treasure of the church is the fourteenth-century bell now displayed on a stand. It is tall and narrow, but carries no inscription. It broke in two in 1939 and was replaced by the bell now to be seen in the tiny bellcote at the west end.

COOLING. These simple fourteenth-century benches with poppy-head ends are among the earliest permanent wooden seats to be found in any English church.

COOLING, St James

The churchyard at Cooling is famous to readers of Dickens as the setting for the opening scenes of *Great Expectations*. By the tower are 'Pip's Graves', a group of thirteen eighteenth-century bodystones that Dickens described so well. The church is thirteenth century in date and is surprisingly large for so small a village. Since 1978 it has been owned by the Churches Conservation Trust, and cared for by local residents. At the back of the church is a series of three fourteenth-century benches – some of the earliest seats in existence. The chancel is particularly lavish and is arcaded with Purbeck marble shafts of thirteenth-century date. The arcading on the south side incorporates three sedilia and a fine double piscina, although the nineteenth-century raising of the floor level has made a nonsense of the composition. The tiny vestry gives the impression of a grotto, its walls being lined with hundreds of cockle shells. The fine east window is a good example of the work of Clayton and Bell.

CRANBROOK, St Dunstan

This church grew from a small Saxo-Norman structure in the fourteenth century, using profits from the English cloth-making industry which was based in the town. It is a large church with several unique features, the most important of which is a font for full adult immersion. This was built under a small stone staircase that leads to a room over the south porch. In reality it was like an upright coffin, constructed in 1710 by the then parson, John Johnson, but it seems only to have been used on one occasion. There are very few of these features to be found in England. A table at the back of the church is made from the upturned sounding board of the eighteenth-century pulpit. The very fine carved Royal Arms of George II were given in 1756. In the north aisle is a collection of sixteenth-century stained glass depicting coats of arms of the Guilford family, and some nice windows by Kempe.

CRAYFORD, St Paulinus

This is one of the most unusual churches in Kent. As a result of rebuildings in the fourteenth century the church has a twin nave leading to a single chancel – the arcade ending oddly in the centre of the chancel arch. Only two other churches in England have this form of plan. Apart from the odd appearance this church is also a good place to study tufa – indicative of Norman work, as are the blocked twelfth-century windows that may still be seen. Many furnishings, including the pulpit, date from the years immediately following a serious fire in the early seventeenth century. There are many good memorials. Particularly impressive is the Draper memorial of 1674 which shows a stillborn son at the base. Another monument commemorates Lady Shovell, widow of Sir Cloudesley Shovell, the famous admiral. Their house, May Place, stood in the parish. Stained glass has not been lucky at Crayford. The medieval glass was lost in a gunpowder explosion in 1864 and its replacements lost in the Second World War. There are several modern windows by Hugh Easton – his symbol, the windvane, being clearly displayed.

CRUNDALE, St Mary

Nave, chancel, north aisle and tower stand in a superb downland setting far from any village. The church is of Norman origin, as can be seen from the surviving window in the north wall of the nave. The semi-circular arches of the two-bay arcade are also late Norman. In the eighteenth century the fine reredos with a scrolly pediment and the altar rails were installed. Also in the

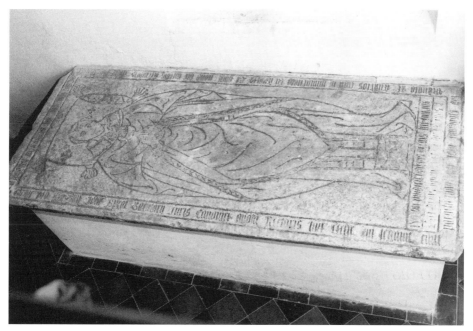

CRUNDALE. The animated fifteenth-century effigy of John Sprot, carved in alabaster, shows him wearing his vestments with his head on an enormous pillow.

chancel is a nice single sedile under a carved canopy. The east window is entirely a nineteenth-century creation. The rood loft stairway survives. The narrow north aisle contains a handsome tomb chest to John Sprot (d. 1466), removed here from the chancel. It is an incised design on an alabaster slab. Sprot wears vestments and holds a chalice with the host displayed. His head rests on a pillow decorated with two little Bottonee crosses. It is a pity that it was not always mounted on a tomb chest as parts of the design have been worn away by the feet of centuries.

CUXTON, St Michael

A fine example of a church that has been extended. The north wall of the nave is Norman, with the original quoins of local tufa showing clearly. There are few churches that have three quoins showing as well as they do here. The chancel has been lengthened almost to the edge of the escarpment, while at the other end a fifteenth-century tower has been added, cut into the hillside. There is a well-known local rhyme – 'If you should find a church miswent, go

71

to Cuxton in Kent' – which derives from the fact that the church is orientated more to the south than the east. In the Middle Ages churches were laid out on the date of their patronal festival and on St Michael's day (29 September) the sun rises further south, which probably accounts for the orientation. There is a good holy water stoup in the porch and remains of the rood loft staircase. In the splay of a north window are the patterns of vine leaf murals, similar to those in nearby Leybourne.

DARTFORD, *Holy Trinity*

The south-west corner of the church was cut away in the eighteenth century for road widening, leaving a very strange 'main front' on view. The oldest part of the building is the northern tower which is twelfth century in date. Although the building has suffered from frequent floods and a powerful nineteenth-century restoration it contains much of interest. At the east end of the south chapel is one of the largest wall paintings in Kent, depicting St George and the Dragon. It dates from the fifteenth century. Also of note for its size is the colossal Royal Arms of George III which hangs in the north chapel. Underneath it stands the tomb of John Spilman, famous for opening the first Kent paper mill in the town at the end of the sixteenth century. Many other monuments from the eighteenth and nineteenth centuries adorn the walls, including a bronze tablet to Richard Trevithick. There is an unusual two-storey medieval vestry at the east end of the south chapel. A modern window designed by Derek Hicks (1992) commemorates local historian Geoff Porteus and shows features of local interest including the heath and eponymous warbler.

DITTON, *St Peter ad Vincula*

In a picturesque position to the west of a large green, this is a tiny two-cell church of twelfth-century date with a fourteenth-century tower. There is much use of tufa in the quoins and some very clear herringbone masonry on the south side. The church was restored in 1859 by Scott which has given the building a distinctive 'cleaned out' feeling inside. The north nave window has fragments of fourteenth-century glass, including two very stilted angels swinging censers. The nave has a good selection of hanging wall monuments and a very elegant benefactions board. An unusual sight is the lead plaque on the nave wall that was removed from the tower roof in 1859. It has a picture of a ship of Nelson's time scratched on it – a very crude representation at that – and is probably not by a seaman returned home as local legend asserts. The good east window of 1910 is by Kempe and Tower.

DODDINGTON. The much-altered medieval church showing the unusual battlemented and weatherboarded west tower.

DODDINGTON, The Beheading of St John the Baptist

An enchanting church set in a wooded churchyard on the edge of a steep valley. The building displays much of medieval interest due to minimal nineteenth-century interference. The most important feature is the small stone prayer desk next to the westernmost window of the chancel. This window is of the low side variety – the desk proving the window's part in devotional activities. The nearby thirteenth-century lancet windows have a series of wall paintings in their splays, while opposite is a fine medieval screen complete with canopy over the priests' seats. There is also an excellent example of a thirteenth-century hagioscope that gives a view of the main altar from the south aisle, which was a structural addition to the original building. The south chancel chapel belonged to the owners of Sharsted Court and contains a fine series of memorials to them. Most of the stained glass is nineteenth century – some of very good quality indeed. Outside there is a good tufa quoin on the north wall of the nave and a short weatherboarded tower.

73

DOVER, *St Mary in the Castle*

From the seventeenth to nineteenth centuries this atmospheric church was a roofless ruin. This goes some way to explaining its Victorian character today. The main walls date from the tenth century when the church was built adjacent to the Roman pharos within the earthworks of Dover Castle. In 1860 Scott brought the church back into use and his are the roof, windows and doors. Where the rubble stonework and re-used Roman tile had decayed Scott replaced it with uncompromising brick. The window surrounds were designed as before – to such an extent that if we did not have access to early photographs we would assume they were original. In 1889 William Butterfield covered the inside walls with a series of mosaics that give the church the impression of a huge bathroom. Some earlier features still manage to peep through the Victorian veil, especially the blocked south doorway of tall Saxon proportions and the thirteenth-century two-seater sedilia and double piscina in the chancel. The church is open to visitors to Dover Castle.

DOVER, *St Mary the Virgin*

In the heart of the town with a prominent twelfth-century tower. From the outside it is obvious that much work was carried out in the nineteenth century. The church has major connections with the Lord Wardens of the Cinque Ports and is much used for ceremonial services. The western bays of the nave with their low semi-circular arches are contemporary with the tower, while the pointed arches to the east are entirely nineteenth century. The scale and choice of stone is entirely wrong, although the carving is very well done. However the east end, with its tall narrow lancet windows, is not so successful. The Royal Arms, of the reign of William and Mary, are of carved and painted wood, with a French motto – Jay Maintendray – instead of the more usual Dieu et Mon Droit. The church was badly damaged in the Second World War, but one of the survivors was the typical Norman font of square Purbeck marble construction. One of the more recent additions to the church is the *Herald of Free Enterprise* memorial window of 1989 designed by Frederick Cole.

DYMCHURCH, *Sts Peter and Paul*

It is difficult to think of Dymchurch without recalling Dr Syn – the smuggling clergyman invented by Russell Thorndike. Yet when one visits this church, standing just off the main coast road within earshot of amusement arcades and holiday chalets, it suddenly hits you that Dr Syn was no more than a storybook hero and that here is real history, unchanged by developments around it. The church is of Norman date, structurally altered in the nineteenth century when the widened nave and little west tower were built. There are some decorated style windows and one thirteenth-century lancet. The east window – which contains good glass of 1927 – has a very slightly pointed arch indicating late Norman work. However, the best original Norman stonework is the chancel arch, which is a tall and wide structure with simple shafting and zigzag moulding. Either side of the arch are recesses for side altars, and in the south wall another recess, showing the remains of thirteenth-century painting, may have served another altar.

EASTCHURCH, *All Saints*

A complete rebuild of 1431, using a few windows from the previous building. The rood screen is the greatest treasure, running the whole width of the building including the aisles, a total of 46 ft. It has a modern cresting to replace its original loft which has been dismantled. The north and south chapels are not as long as the chancel and each is connected to the latter by a hagioscope. On the outside of the church the change in stonework between the ragstone walls and flint battlements is a very striking feature. There is good stained glass of the nineteenth and twentieth centuries including a south window of 1912 by Karl Parsons to commemorate one of the first flying fatalities: Eastchurch was the home of early aviation in England.

EAST MALLING, *St James*

A large and light church with much of interest. The base of the tower is Norman with original windows, while its top stage is fourteenth century. The rest of the church is a fourteenth-century rebuild of a thirteenth-century structure. Much alteration occurred at the end of the nineteenth century but this was done in a most sympathetic way and forms an interesting standard by which to judge other local restorations. The Lady Chapel has a low reredos by Comper (1926), while its charming panelled ceiling is of early fifteenth-century date. The east window in the chapel has good mid-fourteenth-century tracery of three pointed lancets subdivided by quatrefoils and mouchettes and divided by trefoils, one of the most pleasing designs of the period. There is a fine fifteenth-century font cover and many seventeenth- and eighteenth-century mural tablets.

EAST PECKHAM OLD CHURCH. The fifteenth-century windows, south porch and rendered tower are unmistakable, even though the character of this church was completely altered by the addition of a slate roof in the nineteenth century.

EAST PECKHAM, St Michael

The medieval church was superseded by a new church in the village in 1842, but remains in good repair being maintained today by the Churches Conservation Trust. In many ways it is the typical Kentish church, showing work of many different periods and many monuments to remind us of former inhabitants. As in some other local churches the north aisle is the primary one, even though the church is entered from the south. The restoration by diocesan architect Joseph Clarke in 1857 was rather heavy-handed and provided a veritable sea of oak pews. In contrast the south chapel, which belonged to Roydon Hall, has a nice unrestored atmosphere, as does the south porch which shows an abundance of medieval (and later) graffiti. At the lychgate is the famous stable used by nineteenth-century congregations.

EASTWELL, St Mary

One of the few ruined churches in the county, St Mary's stands in a well-kept churchyard on the edge of Eastwell Park Lake. Only the west tower is intact and shows in its lower stage one of the unusual inset flint crosses. To the south of the tower is a nineteenth-century chapel built to house the monument to Lady Winchelsea, which can now be seen in the Victoria & Albert Museum. A stone table marks the burial place of Richard Plantagenet, the illegitimate son of Richard III, who is reputed to have lived in the house which still stands to the east of the churchyard. His burial is recorded in the church register of December 1550. The church was built almost entirely of chalk blocks which, following the construction of the lake in 1841, started to soak up water. This eventually resulted in the total collapse of the church in 1951. The ruins are now maintained by the Friends of Friendless Churches, a national charity, both as a place of pilgrimage and a historic monument.

EDENBRIDGE, Sts Peter and Paul

A fairly small thirteenth- and fourteenth-century church that has been lovingly tended. The building consists of nave, chancel, south aisle and chapel. The latter dates from the fifteenth century and was built to contain the tomb of Richard Martyn (d. 1499). It replaced an earlier chapel that had been dedicted to St John the Baptist. In the nineteenth century Martyn's tomb was removed, but one panel from it has been set into the east wall behind the altar. The rood loft staircase survives at the north side of the chancel arch, in front of which is a good heavy Jacobean pulpit on a modern base. There are Royal Arms of the reign of George I. A corner has been cut off the pier at the north-west corner of the Martyn chapel and probably formed a hagioscope before the chapel was built in its present form. The main east window is of early twentieth-century date and derives from a drawing by Scott of the medieval window that survived until a mid-nineteenth-century local architect replaced it. It contains glass by Morris and Co. of 1909, originally meant for the neighbouring church of Crockham Hall where John Storr, whose memory it commemorates, lived.

ELHAM, St Mary

The church stands in the square removed from the main road. The flint rubble construction and severe restoration of the exterior does not look welcoming, but the interior is most appealing with plenty of light flooding through the clerestory windows. The rectangular piers of both north and south arcades with their painted arches and boldly carved stops are of late twelfth-century date. Between them hang some eighteenth-century text boards. The character of the church is given in the main by late nineteenth- and early twentieth-century work. The high altar has four painted panels by John Ripley Wilmer in Pre-Raphaelite style, executed in 1907. At the opposite end of the church are the organ loft, font cover and baptistry, all designed by F.C. Eden, who restored the church in the early 1900s. He also designed the west window of the south aisle as part of a larger scheme which was not completed. In the south chancel wall are two windows of great curiosity. One contains a fifteenth-century figure of St Thomas à Becket while the other shows figures of David and Saul. This dates from the nineteenth century and was painted by Frank Wodehouse who was the then vicar's brother. The face of David was based on that of Mme Carlotta Patti, the opera singer, while Gladstone and Disraeli can be identified hovering in the background! It is a shame that it has deteriorated badly.

ELMSTED, St James

An extremely worthwhile church in remote countryside. The tower is an unusual shape, being almost twice as wide as it is deep and capped by a wooden upper storey with stumpy spire. The church consists of nave, aisles, chancel and equal length chapels. The nave is Norman: the original arch to the tower is still recognizable although a fourteenth-century replacement has been built inside it. At the same time the present arcade was built on the existing piers. In the north aisle is a medieval vestry screen, in front of which is a Norman font. There are very fine altar rails, each baluster looking like an eighteenth-century candlestick. Between the main altar and chapel is a simple thirteenth-century sedilia. The south chapel altar has a twelfth-century mensa which was discovered in the churchyard in 1956. The east window (1880) commemorates Arthur Honeywood who was killed in the Afghan war – only a dog survived and was given an award by Queen Victoria! Honeywood's ancestor, Sir John (d. 1781), is also remembered in the church by a marble bust signed by Scheemakers.

FAIRFIELD, St Thomas à Becket

The most memorable of churches, it stands completely isolated, with neither a tombstone nor a tree to keep it company. It was reconstructed in 1912 which detracts a little from its antiquarian interest, but this interferes very

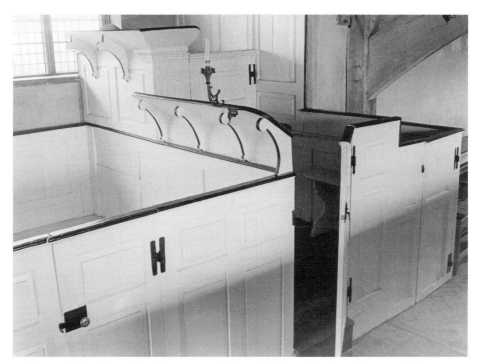

FAIRFIELD. The white-painted box pews and three-decker pulpit that add so much character to this homely little church. The lowest pew, at the back, is for the clerk, the one with open door for the priest and the upper deck for him to preach his sermon!

little with the visual appearance of the interior which is somewhat reminiscent of a farmhouse kitchen! The walls are of bare woodwork and the little square windows allow plenty of light to bathe the white painted box pews and matching three-decker pulpit. The low beam which runs in place of a chancel arch adds much character to the building. As a whole the church probably dates from the medieval period, but it would be impossible to put a date to it in view of the rebuildings.

FARNINGHAM, Sts Peter and Paul

A two-cell thirteenth-century church to which a three-stage tower was added in the fifteenth century. In the churchyard is the Nash Mausoleum of 1778, built in Portland stone. Inside the church all is light and airy with a crownpost roof supported by prominent wall posts. The arch to the tower is Tudor in date and may be slightly later than the tower itself. Under the arch stands the excellent

Seven Sacrament font of fifteenth-century date. It represents Confirmation, Penance, Holy Communion, Extreme Unction, Ordination, Marriage and Baptism. Only one other Seven Sacrament font exists outside East Anglia (at Nettlecombe in Somerset). In the 1830s the vicar's son, Charles Winston, was establishing himself as an expert on medieval glass and designed several windows for Farningham. The finest is the small figure of an archbishop behind the pulpit. Winston based it on the figure of Archbishop Simon de Mepham which he saw in Meopham church, and which has since been destroyed.

FAVERSHAM, St Mary

An extraordinary building comprising a medieval chancel and transepts, eighteenth-century nave and nineteenth-century tower and spire. Despite heavy-handed restorations of the nineteenth century – by Scott and Christian – which have resulted in loss of character, there is much to see. The fourteenth-century transepts are aisled – a most unusual feature in an ordinary parish church. The medieval authorities probably decided to invest in a lavish building to counteract the pulling power of the famous abbey which stood to the east. One of the pillars of the north transept has a series of contemporary small paintings of biblical scenes. You are advised to take a pair of binoculars to see them to advantage. The stalls in the chancel have misericords with a good selection of carved armrests, and there is also a crypt and an unforgettable east window of 1911.

FAWKHAM, St Mary

A two-cell rendered and much-tidied-up church of great charm. At what stage the chancel arch was removed is not known, but now the chancel and nave are divided by a wooden twentieth-century screen. On the north wall of the nave is a thirteenth-century mural of Christ in Majesty – the most impressive for its date in Kent. In the south wall is a Norman piscina and a good fourteenth-century tomb recess. Within the chancel hangs a wall monument to Dorcas and John Watter (d. 1625) of carved alabaster. The two figures face each other across a double prayer desk under their complicated armorial bearings. Beneath is a tightly written inscription recording the fact that John founded a charity to provide overcoats. It is one of the prettiest monuments of the period. In the nearby window are some fragments of medieval glass – including a selection of de Fawkeham armorial shields – and a nice fourteenth-century piece of St Anne teaching the Virgin. These pieces were reset into plain glass in 1930.

FOLKESTONE, *Holy Trinity*

A memorable nineteenth-century church designed in 1868 by Ewan Christian – quite unlike his first ever church at Hildenborough twenty-five years earlier. Built of ragstone rubble it has an octagonal tower and short spire over the chancel. It was an expensive building costing over £13,000 and paid for entirely by the Earl of Radnor, who was busily turning Folkestone from a fishing harbour into a holiday resort. The interior is of brick with Bath stone dressings and has a barrel vaulted wooden ceiling. There is an excellent wrought-iron screen between nave and chancel surmounted by bronze angels. The eastern apse has a series of lancets filled with good quality glass. The reredos beneath dates from 1889 and shows Christ in Glory. It is one of the largest pieces of Victorian work in the county. At the other end of the church stands the font – a whopping piece which incorporates many types of English and foreign marble. There is a carved cover to match!

FOLKESTONE, *St Mary*

A superb location in a leafy churchyard away from the busy shopping centre, and yet much more of a town church than that of a seaside resort. It was originally a thirteenth-century building, but so much has happened to it that today we are left with the impression of a Victorian interior. Excellent stained glass by Kempe, mosaics by Carpenter and paintings by Hemming show the enthusiasm of Canon Woodward, vicar from 1851 to 1898. His efforts encouraged others to donate money to beautify the building in an almost continuous restoration that lasted right into the twentieth century. They were spurred on by the discovery, in 1885, of the bones of St Eanswythe, in a lead casket which had been set into the sanctuary wall. She founded a convent in the town in the seventh century and died at the age of twenty-six.

FORDWICH, *St Mary*

What a surprise to find a church in this part of the county that was not over-restored by the Victorians! What makes it even more unusual is that Fordwich is a town church, rather than a village one. The nave is filled with box pews and leads to a chancel of exceptional length. There is no difference in floor level. The modern east window is by Martin Travers and is more typical of his work than his other windows in Kent at Temple Ewell and Barham. At the west end is the tower arch with a steep ladder leading to the bells. The nave has a frightening lean to the north, possibly caused by a thirteenth-century flooding of the nearby river. Opposite the font is a unique monument which consists of an arcaded table of nineteen pillars sitting under a tiled roof. It has no inscription, but must have belonged to someone of note.

FRINSTED, St Dunstan

Not for those wishing to find a medieval church, although there is evidence of an old building here in a Norman window and crownpost roof. It is interesting that the nineteenth-century work carried out first by Hussey (1856) and then by Scott (1870) for the Pemberton Leigh family is in complete contrast to the work commissioned at nearby Kingsdown by the family at the same time (see separate entry). The second restoration included the wonderful stencilling of the church, to the designs of G.G. Scott Jr. The majority of the furnishings are also Victorian and show the quality that only a fortune could buy in post-industrialized England.

GODMERSHAM, St Laurence

A simple, well-cared-for church which has an extremely complicated building history. The nave and western half of the chancel are Saxon in date, although there are no surviving architectural details of this period. Early in the twelfth century a northern tower with small apsidal chapel was added to the north of the nave. This has recently been restored and its round headed windows may be clearly seen. From the same period dates the remarkable stone carving of an archbishop that is now displayed in the chancel. It may be Archbishop Theobold (d. 1162) or Becket (d. 1170) and could have formed part of a tomb in Canterbury Cathedral. The church was restored by Butterfield in the 1860s. His is the nice rood screen, painted by Gibbs, the angular font of Devonshire marble and the design for the east window. Fine Minton tiles were put in the sanctuary – the medieval tiles gathered up and carefully placed on the window-sill to preserve them. The twentieth century has done much to build upon Butterfield's restoration, including the fine south aisle east window by Kempe and Tower of 1923.

GOODNESTONE, Holy Cross

A large and eminently satisfactory village church. The old part – north aisle of fourteenth-century date and tower of the fifteenth century – was enlarged in 1839 by a rebuilt nave and chancel. The architects were Rickman and

Hussey, pioneers of the nineteenth-century Gothic Revival. The exterior is of knapped flints with stone dressings. Inside all is light and of a piece with an elaborate and dignified chancel. In the north aisle is the monument by Scheemakers to Sir Brook Bridges (d. 1717) who built Goodnestone Park, the gardens of which abut the churchyard. There are small pieces of medieval glass, but by far the most impressive window is at the east end of the north aisle, dated and signed E.S. 1899, showing St Gregory and the Slave Boys.

GOUDHURST, St Mary

Seen from afar Goudhurst is Kent's answer to Rye – a small hilltop village over which broods the lovely church. Its west tower, dating from the seventeenth century, is rather low, but the honey-coloured sandstone is particularly beautiful. We enter the church through the tower, and are impressed by the way in which the width and height combine to make such a noble structure. There are two remarkably fine wooden effigies dating from the sixteenth century, carved and painted and set into a purpose-built bay window. Nearby, in the south chapel, the walls are crammed with monuments and there are three brasses, one of which is covered by a stone canopy – not particularly grand but unexpected and functional.

GRAIN, St James

A small and remote church at the end of the Hoo Peninsula. The usual two-cell Norman church was extended and partially rebuilt in the late twelfth century by the addition of north and south aisles, the introduction of reredos niches for the nave altars and new windows in the chancel. The aisles were demolished in the early nineteenth century, but the blocked arcades are still clearly visible. The reredos niches are both painted with thirteenth-century five-petalled flowers, while the southern one also shows the figure of a bearded bishop. There are the remains of two Norman windows in the nave, and a group of thirteenth-century coffin lids. Despite its medieval size the church did not have a tower until the present one was built in 1905. It tries very hard, and is built in the right architectural style, but the fact that it is shorter than the nave means that it is a rather poor relation to others in the area. Over the south door is an unusual piece of carved stone representing a Sheila-na-gig, or pagan goddess of reproduction, displaying more than a lady should!

GRAVENEY, All Saints

The Victorians did not leave too much of a mark here, for the mellow red tiles, box pews and ledger slabs remain. There is a heavy medieval rood screen and empty north and south aisles which allow us to appreciate the building as it would have originally appeared. In the north aisle is a memorial brass to John Martyn (d. 1436) with cathedral-like proportions, being over 56 in long.

HARBLEDOWN, St Michael

Most people visit the chapel of St Nicholas Hospital in Harbledown, which is just as much a place of pilgrimage today as it was in the Middle Ages. However, the nearby church of St Michael is full of character despite the fact that it dates in the main from 1880. The south aisle is part of the original Norman church – one blocked window survives – and there is a damaged thirteenth-century piscina. There is also an unusual piece of carved stone of uncertain age which represents two bulls fighting, with a sun above them. The architect for the enlargement of 1880 was J.P. St Aubyn – never the most sensitive of architects. There is some pleasing nineteenth- and twentieth-century glass including a rare representation of the Search for the Holy Grail.

HARRIETSHAM, St John the Baptist

A noble church which stands well away from the main road in a very large churchyard. The memorable feature is the second, or north, tower that stands behind the chancel. This is of Norman date, thus predating the present west tower by three hundred and fifty years. There are good pieces of tufa visible on the exterior. The chancel is thirteenth century, with three widely spaced lancets forming the east window, while the nave is mainly fourteenth century in date. The south chapel displays blocked two-light windows that were made redundant in order to accommodate seventeenth-century monuments within. The stained glass is a mixed bag – the best being the twentieth-century composition of Our Lady and Child in the north-east chancel lancet. Below, in front of the altar, is a veritable carpet of medieval tiles, no doubt collected from other parts of the building. The Royal Arms of George III dated 1795 hang over the south door while the nearby Norman font attracts much attention. It is of local Bethersden marble with a heavy cable moulding around the rim and is quite different in character to any other twelfth-century font in the county.

HARTY, St Thomas

Harty is a small island adjoining the south-eastern corner of the Isle of Sheppey. The church is small and rustic, consisting of nave, north aisle, chancel and south chapel. There is evidence of the Norman period in the tufa arch high in the north wall. The south chapel was built in the fifteenth century and now contains the greatest treasure of the church – a fourteenth-century wooden chest or Flemish Kist. It is carved on the front with two knights jousting. Following its recent theft and subsequent discovery a superb metal screen has been installed that now secures the chapel and allows the visitor to gaze at this venerable object. A further modern addition is the south nave window which shows the eponymous sheep on which this island still depends. The rood screen is fourteenth century and returns along the north wall of the nave and into the north aisle. The original entrance to the loft is still visible. In the sanctuary is a fifteenth-century image niche which may well have held a statue of Thomas à Becket – for this church was on the pilgrim route by boat from London to Canterbury.

HASTINGLEIGH, St Mary the Virgin

At the end of narrow lanes. A small simple building of tower, nave, wide south aisle and chancel. The nave is Norman and displays a very narrow twelfth-century window high in its north wall. The rest of the church appears to be thirteenth century – the two-bay south arcade dating from this period. There are traces of later wall paintings in the aisle. The rood screen is fifteenth century and leads the visitor into an exceptionally long and light chancel whose floor level is lower than that of the nave. A south window contains sixteenth-century armorial glass while a northern lancet shows excellent grisaille glass of the thirteenth century.

HAWKINGE, St Michael

The churchyard almost tumbles away from the church to the south and is not enhanced by the plain building whose dark flints and unbroken roofline make for an undistinguished scene. However, once inside the door the whole atmosphere changes. The porch is most welcoming – its rubble walls whitewashed and its benches highly varnished. Its inner door is low and has an amusing ventilation panel built into it. The interior of the church is functional. Polished pews contrast with white walls, the whole under a tall kingpost roof. There is no division between nave and chancel. The windows in the nave have extra wide splays, but it is the chancel windows that really catch our attention. The east wall contains what looks as if it should be the familiar three narrow lancet arrangement, but the central light is missing. In its place is a plinth on which there would originally have been a statue. This is matched outside by a large buttress to stop the church falling down the hill. In the south wall of the chancel is a low side window which ends in a ledge near the floor, and there are two piscinae – one in the usual position, the other at the corner of the sedilia.

HEADCORN, Sts Peter and Paul

A church of the Perpendicular period whose size reflects the medieval wealth brought here by the cloth trade. The base of the rood screen is early sixteenth century, and some fragments of glass of the same date survive in the tracery of a north window. The pulpit is a curious piece knocked up from pieces of old woodwork. Yet for woodwork the outstanding feature of Headcorn is the roof, which is accepted as one of the most accomplished mid-fourteenth-century structures in the country. Also of good quality are the Royal Arms of George III painted by J. Adams in 1808. There is a large south porch of the fifteenth century with an upper room which has a small window into the church – a sure sign that this was a priest's parvise, and not just storage space.

HERNE, St Martin

A large, impressive and little-known building of fourteenth-century date. Although nineteenth-century restorations have left us with a church that displays little patina it still contains much of interest. The chancel screen dates from 1872 and provides good comparison with the fourteenth-century screen of the north chapel which, unusually, has two east windows. The sedilia in the chancel is a series of three multi-cusped arches descending to the west – although the Victorian floor level makes a nonsense of their height. The nearby piscina is fifteenth century. The east window and theatrical reredos are nineteenth century and form an interesting ensemble. There are some fine misericords incorporated into the Victorian stalls. On the north chancel wall is a good Easter Sepulchre – the memorial of Sir John Fyneux (d. 1525). The north chapel was a chantry foundation with its own priest and is connected to the chancel by a two-bay arcade and hagioscope. The rood loft stairway to the south of the chancel arch indicates that the screen did not run the full width of the church and that each of the chapel screens was a separate construction.

HERNHILL, St Michael

Like many medieval churches with this dedication, St Michael's stands on a hill, with fine views across the Swale estuary. A complete fifteenth-century church, it is obviously much loved, and while it contains little of outstanding interest is a typical village church of chancel, nave, aisles and substantial west tower. In the south aisle are three accomplished windows painted by the vicar's wife in the nineteenth century. There is a medieval rood screen and nineteenth-century screens elsewhere. In the churchyard is a memorial plaque to John Thom, a.k.a. Sir William Courtenay, who raised an unsuccessful rebellion in nearby Bossenden Wood in May 1838 and who is buried in the churchyard.

HEVER, St Peter

Near the grounds of Hever Castle, medieval home of the Bullen family. Sandstone construction with a nice west tower and spire. There is a prominent chimney to the north chapel, although this is not the usual Victorian addition, but a Tudor feature, whose little fireplace may be seen in the chapel! The church contains much of interest including a nineteenth-century painting of Christ before Caiphas by Reuben Sayers and another from the school of Tintoretto. The stained glass is all nineteenth and twentieth century and includes a wonderfully evocative east window (1898) by Burlisson and Grylls with quite the most theatrical sheep! The south chancel window of St Peter is by Hardman and dated 1877. In the north chapel is a fine tomb chest which displays the memorial brass of Sir Thomas Bullen (d. 1538), the father of Queen Anne Boleyn. Just around the corner is a good, though rather insubstantial, seventeenth-century pulpit with sounding board.

HIGH HALSTOW, St Margaret

A late medieval ragstone church on an exposed hilltop. The square-headed clerestory windows let in large amounts of light on to the thirteenth-century arcade. The font is also thirteenth century in date and there are faint traces of wall paintings. No stained glass and a reordering of 1984 have created an atmosphere for modern worship – quite different to the appearance of the building in 1399 when William Groby, the then rector, died. His half length memorial brass mounted on the wall was apparently discovered on a pile of rubbish during nineteenth-century rebuilding work! Outside all the details are much weathered and the whole building has had to be substantially repaired following storm damage. The west tower is substantially an eighteenth-century structure with lots of brick patching and buttressing. The only single part of the medieval building not to have suffered much rebuilding is the south porch of fifteenth-century date, with an ornate image niche over the doorway.

HIGHAM, St Mary

Difficult to find, but more than worth the effort. It consists of a Norman nave and chancel to which a south aisle and chapel were added in the mid-fourteenth century. The aisle and chapel are now laid out as the main nave and chancel. The exterior has wonderful striped walls, like a smaller version of nearby Cliffe, and the fourteenth-century south door is the highly carved original. Inside the contemporary pulpit is one of the earliest in the county with six carved traceried panels. Behind it is a fifteenth-century rood screen, which, despite the loss of its loft, is a surprising survival. In the north-east corner of the Lady Chapel is a table tomb whose top is made up from the

HIGHAM OLD CHURCH. The fourteenth-century south aisle which shows the striped alternate materials of ragstone and flint. The porch is Victorian and protects a wonderful medieval south door.

88

original stone altar slab, or mensa, with its five consecration crosses showing prominently. In the south wall of the same chapel is a medieval aumbry with its original hinged door. The stained glass is all nineteenth and twentieth century – the excellent south chancel window showing the Agony in the Garden is dated 1863 but by an unidentified artist. Of the same date is the tortoise stove in the north aisle, which displays on its lid the motto 'Slow but sure combustion'. The church is excellently maintained by the Churches Conservation Trust – the congregation worshipping in a replacement church in the village, built in 1860 by E.W. Stephens of Maidstone.

HINXHILL, St Mary

One of the best churches in which to see thirteenth-century simplicity. That the church was always poor can be seen by the fact that there is no chancel arch – rather more a timber division – using the cheaper local materials in

HIGHAM OLD CHURCH. The rood screen and pulpit which both date from the fourteenth century. The little rustic traceried panels are typical of work of this period.

place of more expensive imported stone. In fact there is *some* imported stone here – a font of Caen stone and a really elaborate hanging memorial to Robert Edolph (d. 1632) to the north of the altar, with almost life-size figures. The Royal Arms of George III are signed by J. Marten. There is a thirteenth-century piscina and fourteenth-century aumbry nearby. On the outside of the nave south wall you can find a good selection of medieval graffiti, possibly carved by pilgrims, and in the spring the churchyard is full of snowdrops.

HOLLINGBOURNE, All Saints

There was considerable damage caused to this church in an earthquake of 1382. The medieval accounts survive so we know that 48s 2d was spent on the rebuilding. Little can have changed to the structure since that time, except the construction of a north chapel in 1638. This chapel has a charming pattern of flint flushwork triangles in a horizontal course below the battlements. It contains one of the most interesting seventeenth-century monuments in Kent – to commemorate Lady Elizabeth Culpepper (d. 1638), carved and signed by Edward Marshall. The detail is amazing and the cord that connects her ring and wrist is always pointed out to visitors. The rest of the church was restored early in the career of George Gilbert Scott Jr in 1876 (see also Frinsted) and retains its patina of age unimaginable in a restoration by Scott Sr. The pulpit is early seventeenth century and dates from a few years after the much crocketed font cover. There are three signed monuments by Rysbrack and a tall crownpost roof of good construction in the nave.

HOO ST WERBURGH, St Werburgh

An architecturally interesting church despite poor quality nineteenth-century restorations. The tower is Norman with a fourteenth-century top and spire – with very clear pilaster buttresses and a round-headed window in its lower levels. The nave and aisle are thirteenth century in date with the usual round piers. In the chancel is a good example of a fifteenth-century sedilia, the three seats having two columns of polished Bethersden marble separating them. At either end of the hood mould are little monks' heads – possibly referring to the patronage of the church belonging to St Andrew's Priory, Rochester. There is also a good piscina incorporated into the composition. Unfortunately the nineteenth-century reredos, of seven much cusped and pinnacled panels, detracts from the medieval work and cuts across the base of the Perpendicular east window. The church was often used as a navigational aid by ships in the Medway and many monuments and memorials in church and churchyard are connected to seafarers or those who lost their lives at sea.

HORSMONDEN, St Margaret

The best way to see and appreciate this church in its setting is from the south. Unfortunately the church was over-restored in 1867, although it manages to retain some character. The most impressive feature is the soaring tower arch which dates from the fifteenth century. On the floor of the chancel is a beautiful brass of Henry de Grofhurst, dating from about 1340, and the nearby tomb recess in the wall may have been part of the same composition. In the south aisle are two rood loft stairways, which indicates that one must have been superseded by the other at some stage early in the fifteenth century. Over the south door is a bust of John Read – inventor of the stomach pump and round oast house. Twentieth-century fittings include the bright jazzy east and west windows by Rosemary Everett.

HORTON KIRBY, St Mary

As the guidebook says, this is a much mutilated church! It is of late Norman origins, but rebuildings in the fourteenth and nineteenth centuries have left a church that is neither pretty nor inviting. The interior, however, offers the more experienced church-crawler a wealth of detail. The late Norman work may have been done by the same masons who worked at Rochester Cathedral as their masons' marks are identical. The fourteenth-century rebuilding took place as a result of earthquake damage of 1382 (see also Hollingbourne) when the nave collapsed. The work resulted in the demolition of the aisles and the patching up of the chancel. In the early nineteenth century the central tower was rebuilt and the chancel shortened to bring the altar nearer the nave. There is a series of good eighteenth-century wall tablets to the Bathurst family, and two memorial brasses. It may not be the loveliest church in Kent, but it is much loved and deserves more visitors.

HOTHFIELD, St Margaret

Substantially rebuilt after a fire of 1598. The welcoming interior displays no chancel arch, although the doorways in the arcade show where the medieval screen ran the width of the church. The striking east window was designed by Wallace Wood in 1954. There is a good aumbry and piscina nearby. To the north of the chancel stands the excellent tomb chest of Sir John Tufton

(d. 1624). The arcade into which it is built was lowered to allow a semi-circular alabaster ceiling to be inserted to set the composition off. Because it is completely free-standing it is one of the easiest tomb chests in Kent to study, with five sons kneeling on the south side and four daughters on the north . In addition there are complicated coats of arms and an inscription which records the rebuilding of the church by Tufton after the fire. On top of the chest lie Sir John and his wife, with their son Nicholas kneeling between their heads. Much of the monument is still covered with its original paint. The organ, which stands in the south aisle, may be the instrument on which Sir Arthur Sullivan composed 'The Lost Chord'. It originally stood in Hothfield Place where Sullivan was a frequent guest.

HOUGHAM, St Lawrence

In its day this must have been a magnificent church. Its day would have been during the period 1100 to 1150, for a large building was constructed at this time. Even today the remains are impressive. As in many east Kent churches there is no chancel arch. There is a tremendous lean to the south chancel wall. It also shows the blocked arcade to a former south chapel. The north chapel has an impressive east window in Early English style which was copied by the Victorians when they replaced the chancel east window. For once it is possible to compare the Victorian and medieval work almost side by side. While nineteenth-century windows are fine elsewhere in the church this juxta-position at Hougham clearly demonstrates the superiority of the medieval work. By far the most interesting feature at Hougham is the tower. The arch from the nave is particularly lofty and leads into an extremely tall and spacious chamber which can best be described as cavern-like.

HYTHE, St Leonard

A large civic church, as befits one of the original Cinque Ports. Traces of the Norman building may still be seen in the blocked round-headed windows in the north wall of the nave and the excellent Norman arch at the east end of the south aisle. The chancel is thirteenth century in origin, completed by Pearson in 1886. The pulpit is a great piece of Victorian craftsmanship, designed by Street in 1876. The three-light stained glass in the east window is by Wallace Wood and dates from 1951. There are Royal Arms of the reign of William and Mary. The chancel has a triforium gallery, an unexpected find in a parish church. A circular staircase runs from the north-west corner linking the triforium, rood loft and roof. Under the chancel is an interesting processional passage, or ambulatory, which contains hundreds of skulls collected from the churchyard during clearances. It is open to the public during the summer. In the churchyard is the grave of Lionel Lukin, who obtained a patent for his invention – the lifeboat – in 1785.

ICKHAM, St John the Evangelist

The church is entered from the south and is much longer than first impressions indicate. The nave is very dark, for it has no clerestory and is only lit by the outer aisle windows. The chancel, which is long and out of alignment, is most impressive, being built at a much higher level than the nave. There are two transepts, the one on the south partly blocked by the organ which has lovely barley-twist carving. Behind it is an unexpected chapel, possibly built as a chantry by Thomas de Baa who died in 1339. His tomb occupies the south wall and is a good example of its type. What makes this church even more interesting is that there is a 'twin' monument in the north transept to William Heghtesbury who died in 1372 – although this is in a better state of repair.

IGHTHAM, St Peter

The church is built on a steep hillside and displays an interesting brick-built north aisle. The chancel is full of unusual memorials, the most noteworthy of

IGHTHAM. The north aisle, built in 1639, which displays the round-headed windows of the period. The brickwork is laid in alternate courses of headers and stretchers known as English bond.

which is to Sir Thomas Cawne and dates from the end of the fourteenth century. He is wearing armour and chain mail and lies under a canopy beneath a window that forms part of the same composition. In the churchyard is a nice nineteenth-century tomb designed by William Burges. The other monuments of note are all to the Selby family, the most famous of whom is Dorothy Selby (d. 1641) who is reputed to have had a connection with the Gunpower Plot.

IVYCHURCH, *St George*

A large church with little in the way of individual interest, but nevertheless with a great atmosphere. It consists of a fourteenth-century aisled nave with eastern chapels and a substantial west tower. Excellent rustic woodwork includes queenpost roofs, medieval parclose screens to the chapels and

IWADE. A detail of the fourteenth-century east window of the south chapel which shows the Crucifixion.

chancel stalls in collegiate style. The Creed and Commandments hang to either side of the crude east window. The east window of the north aisle is altogether finer, but has been infilled leaving the shape of the tracery visible. Over the south door is a good Royal Arms of George III in a deeply patterned frame. The north aisle is empty, and displays its uneven, unrestored, floor of tile and brick. At the west end of the church is a tremendously powerful tower screen (inscribed 1686 I.G.R.B.C.W) with eight little classical arches either side of a central door.

IWADE, All Saints

Tower, nave, south aisle and chancel hug the slope overlooking the estuary of the River Swale. The tower has clear putlog holes – created when the constructional scaffolding was removed. Several of them have been converted into little windows. The south door is medieval with its original handle of two winged lizards. Also medieval is the rood screen, now to be found in the south aisle. The east window of the south chapel is a good quality fifteenth-century representation of the Crucifixion, although parts of it may be nineteenth-century replacements. The nave roof has been plastered to cut down on draughts, leaving the crownposts to sail into nothingness. When Ewan Christian restored the chancel in the 1870s he removed the plaster from that part of the church. The Royal Arms are of George III and there is a sixteenth-century piscina in the chancel.

KEMSING, St Mary the Virgin

A chocolate-box church in a well-maintained churchyard. The nave is twelfth century in date, rebuilt in the fourteenth century when the present roof was constructed. The chancel is also early but was reconstructed in the sixteenth century. A north aisle was added in 1890. The character of the church derives almost entirely from the nineteenth- and twentieth-century furnishings with which it is blessed. The rood screen is of the correct proportion and design and in the main dates from 1894 with minimal amounts of old woodwork. The wonderful figures on top are of 1908 and were designed by Sir Ninian Comper – the angels balance on their wheels like unicyclists! Comper also designed the wall paintings in the chancel, the altar, reredos and canopy. In the north aisle is an interesting collection of furnishings. There is a painted tile picture of Kemsing by the Kent artist Donald Maxwell, one of only a handful to survive. The central window is of two bishops and is typical of Comper's work, but it does not carry his usual

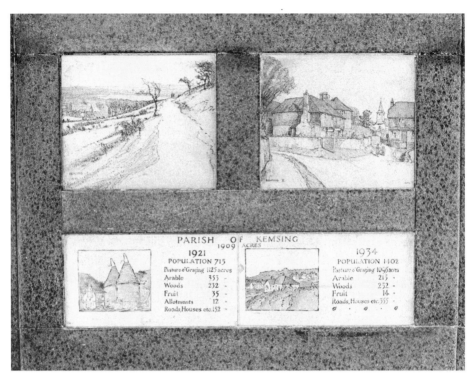

KEMSING. One of the few tiles from Donald Maxwell's series to have survived. It shows the village in his characteristic style, together with details of the population at the time.

signature of a strawberry plant. The west window of the north aisle is by Douglas Strachan, 1935, and is an excellent example of his angular figures. By the font is a bronze Arts and Crafts panel of the Virgin and Child by Henry Wilson, the famous turn-of-the-century designer who lived in a neighbouring village.

KENARDINGTON, St Mary

In a very exposed position overlooking Romney Marsh. The church originally consisted of an aisled nave, chancel with chapels and west tower. In the fourteenth century the building was damaged by a French raiding party and in 1559 struck by lightning. As a result the ruins were patched up to provide a smaller church more suited to the requirements of this small farming community. The bulk of the church was demolished, leaving the former south aisle and chapel to serve as the new church. This means that

KENARDINGTON. The strange eighteenth-century font which would be mistaken for a birdbath if placed in the churchyard!

the north wall is virtually untouched by windows or monuments. On the south wall the original large windows were reduced in size by infilling the outer lights, leaving some excellent 'ghost' tracery visible. The font is a plain oval bowl and would not look out of place as a garden birdbath. Nearby is an oak-panelled screen which bears the date 1717. On the jambs of the main door are some excellent examples of medieval travellers' graffiti.

KILNDOWN, Christ Church

This church is one of the most important Gothic Revival churches in the country. The massive stone and marble gateway leads into the churchyard which contains many memorials to the Beresford Hope family, who paid for this fine building. The impressive interior is full of interesting Victorian furnishings, including a wall pulpit based on the thirteenth-century example that survives at Beaulieu in Hampshire. The stained glass is mostly of German design and much richer than one normally finds in this part of England. Many famous designers were associated with Kilndown, including Salvin, Carpenter and Butterfield, and these early tentative steps towards a fully ecclesiological interior are especially instructive.

KINGSDOWN, *St Catherine*

The church is well known to travellers on the M2, but is difficult to find down a country lane outside Sittingbourne. It is the only surviving Anglican church to have been designed by E.W. Pugin. It was built by Lord Kingsdown in 1861 to replace a medieval church; it is built of ragstone with Bath stone dressings and displays a pretty patterned tile roof. The spire, with lucarnes, presents a very prickly outline. Inside the church the visitor finds one of the most complete Victorian interiors to survive in Kent. The stained glass by Hardman, tiles, metalwork and sculpture are all as Pugin intended. The windows of the chancel have some plain red glass to give a 'holy' atmosphere to the altar. At the opposite end of the church the deeply carved font stands on very solid marble shafts. A few survivals from the old church may be picked out, including some tiles in the vestry and a small sixteenth-century inscription tablet. The church is now cared for by the Churches Conservation Trust.

KINGSTON, *St Giles*

A flint church dating from the early Norman period, when imported stone for quoins was expensive. This is one of the handful of churches in the county where the corners were rudely formed of flint. In the fourteenth century the chancel was extended to the east and a tower added at the west end. Three well-known nineteenth-century designers were involved at Kingston. The east window is by Heaton, Butler and Bayne, the chancel roof by William White and the choir stalls by Norman Shaw. Of medieval date is a plain Perpendicular piscina and a good aumbry, while the pulpit is a typical example of sixteenth-century work.

LAMBERHURST, *St Mary*

A pretty church with views into Sussex. Nave and chancel with a south chapel, south aisle and west tower which is aligned with the aisle – which means that there is no west door. The chancel and chapel were rebuilt in 1870 by Ewan Christian, but he kept the fourteenth-century sedilia which stand between the two. They form a stone bench with two quatrefoil openings cut through the backrests, giving a view into the chapel. To the east there is a tall lancet opening for a piscina with a rectangular aumbry above. The floor has been raised 3ft 6in and the whole church interior reordered. The fine reredos in the south chapel is by Tinworth (1870), while the seventeenth-century pulpit carries the initials of the then rector, Robert Steede. A good Royal Arms of Queen Anne and crownpost roof complete the old furnishings which were further enhanced in 1984 when a window of the Annunciation was installed to the design of John Piper.

LEEDS, St Nicholas

One of the largest twelfth-century towers in Kent. The arch between tower and nave is of three very plain orders with no hint of the usual zigzag moulding of the period, and is so large that a meeting room has recently been built into it. The nave has three bay aisles and short chapels to north and south of the chancel. The outstanding rood screen was partially reconstructed in 1892, and runs the full width of nave and aisles – with the staircase doorways in the south aisle. That the chancel was rebuilt in the sixteenth century may be seen by the plain sedilia through which is cut one of two hagioscopes from chapels to chancel. The north chapel contains some good seventeenth- and eighteenth-century tablets and monuments. The stained

LEEDS. The fifteenth-century rood screen which runs the full width of the church. Unusually the panels take no account of the blank areas of wall between nave and chapels.

glass shows some excellent examples of the work of Heaton, Butler and Bayne (south aisle) while there is an uncharacteristically poor example of the Kempe studio in the north aisle. The church has recently been reordered to provide a spacious, light and manageable interior with excellent lighting and a welcoming atmosphere without damaging the character of the building.

LEIGH, St Mary

The tall tower, which is such a feature of the village, dates only from the nineteenth century. Once inside we can immediately see that the church is much altered from its fourteenth-century origins. The westernmost windows of the nave are of clear glass. This allows us to appreciate the coloured pillar on the north wall which has lost its original aisle, due to a fire in the late fifteenth century. Looking eastwards the illusion is of a much longer building, for the narrow chancel arch takes the eye to a very narrow east window. The best stained glass is that in the south aisle which shows the agricultural year of sowing, ploughing and reaping. At the back of the church is a series of old prints which show the church at various stages over the past two hundred years.

LENHAM, St Mary

A village centre setting where the church is approached from the north. This side shows ragstone and flint construction. Although the building contains work of earlier periods it is on the whole a fourteenth-century structure. The memorable feature is the size of the internal door which fills the tower arch – although it is not as old as it appears. On the south wall of the nave is a faded mural of St Michael. The pulpit is Elizabethan with a slightly later tester that carries the date 1622. Next to the pulpit is a good window in the style of Kempe, signed in the inscription by H.W. Bryans. The other glass is mid-nineteenth century and of poor quality. The lectern, of wood, with nicely carved feet, may be as early as the fourteenth century, and has a crude and rural feel about it. The medieval stalls, which are returned along the west side of the chancel arch, are much restored. On the north wall of the chancel is an extremely strange monument which shows a fourteenth-century priest lying obliquely in two halves! The Royal Arms over the north door date from the reign of Queen Anne.

LEYBOURNE, Sts Peter and Paul

Too close to the main road for its own good and too generously restored in the nineteenth century to have the feeling of great age; yet Leybourne church has some remarkable objects of interest. The west tower, of a completely different texture to the main building, was constructed by Blomfield in 1874. The base of the medieval tower survives within. The nave is Norman in date and has two good windows of this date in the south wall. The westernmost has some fine vineleaf paintings on its deep inner splays. The star attraction of the church is the heart shrine of Sir Roger de Leybourne (d. 1271). This is a small traceried recess of two lights in the base of which stand two caskets, one of which contains Sir Roger's heart. He died on the final crusade to the Holy Land when it was the practice to send just the heart home for burial. The only other heart shrine in Kent is at Brabourne. Fifteen years after his death King Edward I and Queen Eleanor visited his tomb, and they may have given the two iron crowns that hang on the wall nearby. They were discovered bricked up in the wall by the Victorian restorers.

LOWER HALSTOW, St Margaret

Here is a church which really shows its Saxon origins, the south chancel wall displaying the tell-tale herringbone masonry executed in part in Roman tile. The chancel arch and north and south arcades date from the thirteenth century and are simple cut-throughs, with plain piers between. The chancel has internal wall arcading with Bethersden marble shafts. Above the chancel arch hangs a George III Royal Arms while below it can be seen the notches where the rood beam was originally supported. The lead font – of twelfth-century date – is of cast metal with a king and an angel on each of its ten sides. It was discovered in 1921 hidden under plaster. There are the remains of some unclear fourteenth-century wall paintings and a very interesting piece of graffiti – a Persian beast with the head of a man, body of a lion, mane of quills and sting of a scorpion! This can be found on the south nave arcade.

LUDDESDOWNE, Sts Peter and Paul

A church that is often dismissed as being of little interest, yet this thirteenth-century building, so harshly restored in the nineteenth, shows a wide variety of items of interest. There is part of the brass of a knight, Sir James Montacute, that was obviously damaged when the south arcade was rebuilt. The stencilling on the walls and ceiling was executed by Heaton, Butler and

Bayne in 1894, while the excellent reredos of the Last Supper was designed by Christian and carved by Earp in 1873. The nineteenth-century patrons of the living – the Wigans from East Malling – spent enormous sums beautifying this church and creating something of which the Victorians could be proud. Although as part of their work they heightened and repointed the tower it was not completely rebuilt and the medieval rough wooden ladder survives inside.

LULLINGSTONE, St Botolph

This is not a private chapel, and may be visited at all times, even though you have to walk across the private lawn of Lullingstone Castle to reach it. From the south the eighteenth-century alterations made to the two-cell Norman church may be clearly seen. The walls were raised to accommodate an elaborate plaster ceiling, and a south porch was added. Yet these were not the first alterations to have taken place: in the sixteenth century a north chapel

LULLINGSTONE. The two-cell Norman church was altered in the eighteenth century by the raising of the walls using brick and the addition of a porch and spirelet.

was added to the chancel to take the tomb of Sir John Peche (d. 1522) which lies under an arch between chancel and chapel. Sir John was also responsible for building the rood screen, which contains carvings of peach stones as a pun on his name. This screen was embellished in the eighteenth century when a balustrade was added. There are further monuments of note; on the south of the chancel is the large monument to Sir Percyvall Hart (d. 1581) while in the north chapel is the splendid chest tomb of Sir George Hart (d. 1587). It is in complete contrast to the Gothick wall panel commemorating Percyvall Hart (d. 1738) opposite. It is good to know that the Hart Dyke family connection with the church continues, for here true continuity of social history may be studied as in no other Kent church.

LYDD, All Saints

An enormous church, over 200 ft in length with a west tower 132 ft high. At the back of the church are substantial sections of Saxon walling – and early Saxon at that – while at the east end of the church the visitor can see some very recent work, the stonework of the main east window of 1958 by Anthony Swaine. It is an excellent job, brought about by bomb damage. The three lancets that Mr Swaine introduced are fully in keeping with the rest of the building and contemporary in design with the seven-bay arcades of the nave. The glass in the window is by Leonard Walker. In the north chapel is the Stuppeny tomb – a fairly plain tomb chest – around which the bailiff and jurats of the town were formerly elected. Nearby is a medieval cross-legged knight of late thirteenth-century date. In the south aisle is the bust of Anne Russell, which is signed by Flaxman and is probably his earliest recorded monument. The south chapel contains a late thirteenth-century double piscina and the church also contains a large Royal Arms of George II.

LYMINGE, St Mary and St Ethelburga

In the churchyard, west of the present building, are the foundations of the seventh-century church founded by St Ethelburga, daughter of King Ethelbert and Queen Bertha (see Canterbury). The present church is also Saxon and stands north of the original building so that the old north wall is now the south wall of today's church. When the church was founded there was no village, which explains why the present village stands a little removed from the restricted plateau site. The first thing the visitor sees is an enormous flying buttress holding up the south-east corner of the church – the pathway actually runs beneath it! The north aisle was added in the fifteenth century. It is separated from the nave by a three-bay arcade with most unusual piers. The chancel arch is also out of the ordinary and is probably the result of fifteenth-century rebuilding of the Saxon original. A great deal of nineteenth-century work survives, including a good east window and reredos, neither of which detracts from the antiquity and atmosphere of this interesting building.

LYMPNE, St Stephen

Standing next to the medieval castle on the top of a steep slope, the long and rather forbidding church has a unique atmosphere. From the north all appears to be of the thirteenth century, but the sheer mass of the tower gives away the Norman origins of the building. The church is entered through the north aisle. Inside, there are blocked Norman arches on the west face of the tower which indicate that it was originally an outer wall. The thirteenth-century arch which cuts between nave and tower contrasts well with the twelfth-century arch between nave and chancel. There is a good collection of stained glass; particularly appealing is the window which shows St Elizabeth of Hungary, and the east window of 1950 by J.E. Nuttgens.

LYNSTED, Sts Peter and Paul

The church stands close to the road in a dark and sombre churchyard. Inside, the chancel arch is unusual in that the capitals have been cut off to facilitate the construction of the rood loft. The interesting east window of five lights has a very closely set grouping of openings under the canopy. There are two chapels – the north belonging to the Hugessons and the south to the Teynhams. They both contain excellent monuments. The most important commemorates Lord Teynham (d. 1622) and is signed by Epiphanius Evesham. It shows Lord Teynham lying on his back with his widow kneeling under an arch behind him. At the base are relief carvings of their children. The sons have just returned from hunting and the daughters are crying – two of them have little dogs. Opposite this monument is another to his father who died in 1618, altogether a more ordinary composition.

MAIDSTONE, All Saints

One of the widest churches in Kent, dating from the late fourteenth century when it was granted a College of Canons whose buildings still exist nearby. The tower, which stands to the south of the nave, originally had a tall spire, but it was struck by lightning in 1730 and not replaced. The breathtaking scale of the interior – an aisled nave of six bays, chancel and chapels, is somewhat compromised by the severe wooden roofs inserted by Pearson who restored the church in 1886. A good set of Victorian stained glass includes work by Clayton and Bell, Wailes (1861) and Carpronnier (1872). The twenty stalls have excellent misericords, mostly showing coats of arms of those associated with the college. Archbishop Courtenay (d. 1396) is possibly buried in the chancel, and a brass indent to him survives. Set into the fine sedilia is the tomb of John Wotton (d. 1417), the first master of the college. It incorporates a painting of Wotton being presented to Our Lady. Nearby are graffiti associated with a game of noughts and crosses! There are many other monuments including one to John Astley (d. 1639) by court sculptor Edward Marshall. It depicts two men and women in their shrouds. Astley was Master of the Revels to King James and King Charles. There is also a memorial to Sir Charles Booth (d. 1795) signed by Nollekens.

MARDEN, St Michael and All Angels

A picturesque church, especially when viewed from the south, with a little weatherboarded top to its short tower. There was a fire here in 1554, which did great damage to the thirteenth-century building. The south arcade has some finely carved capitals of fourteenth-century date, while there is a contemporary tomb recess in the south chapel. The pretty font cover of the seventeenth century has some of the best Jacobean carving in this part of Kent. The rood loft stairway may be seen in the south-eastern pier. The east window, which depicts the Vision of St John, was designed in 1962 by Patrick Reyntiens. It is one of the finest modern windows in Kent and may be compared to the roughly contemporary glass at Tudeley by Chagall. In spite of its unashamedly modern approach the work here is far more conventional and appropriate for its setting.

MEOPHAM, St John the Baptist

A large fourteenth-century church with a regularity of detail that tells of much nineteenth-century replacement. The tall octagonal piers of the five-bay arcade are capped by a pretty clerestory of small quatrefoils. The wooden pulpit was made for St Margaret's, Westminster, in 1682 and brought here in 1800 by the then vicar who taught at Westminster School. It has charming cherubs' heads, cockle shells and festoons and could go a long way to enlivening a dull sermon! The former chantry chapel of Simon de Mepham (1272–1333), Archbishop of Canterbury, and a fourteenth-century political pawn, is linked to the chancel by an iron-grilled window.

MEREWORTH, St Lawrence

One of the few eighteenth-century churches in Kent, built in 1746 by the 7th Earl of Westmoreland. It is surprising that for so late a date the name of the architect is not known. It is in the style of Colen Campbell who designed the nearby castle, but as he died in 1722 it cannot be by him. The church consists of a tall stone steeple with four urns at the top of the tower. The body of the church is a plain rectangular box consisting of an aisled nave and chancel. Inside is an excellent display of eighteenth-century interior decoration – especially fine being the curved ceiling which is painted with *trompe l'oeil* panels. At the west end is the galleried pew belonging to Mereworth Castle – it has painted organ pipes on its rear wall. The south-west chapel contains memorials brought here from the old church which stood near the castle, including one to a fifteenth-century Lord Bergavenny, and Sir Thomas Fane (d. 1589). The latter monument has a superb top-knot! The church contains much heraldic stained glass of sixteenth-century date, best seen with binoculars early in the morning. Of Victorian date is the excellent Raising of Lazarus window, installed in 1889 by Heaton, Butler and Bayne. In the churchyard is the grave of Charles Lucas, the first man to be awarded the Victoria Cross, while serving on the *Hecla* during the Crimean War.

MERSHAM, St John the Baptist

A pretty, many-gabled church with a fine short shingled spire. The church is a fourteenth-century rebuild of a Norman original that had been enlarged in the late 1200s. On a tie-beam in the chancel is a carved head of Joan, Countess of Kent, who was married to the Black Prince, son of Edward III. There is a fair amount of medieval glass, in the chancel and nave west window. The screens which separate the south chapel from the chancel and south aisle are wonderful examples of seventeenth-century craftsmanship. The base is constructed of solid panels, the upper levels of very closely set barley-twist balusters, and the top is of tall iron spikes. The south chapel contains many memorials to the Knatchbull family. Above the screen is a corbel of possibly thirteenth-century date which depicts a bishop, and which might be part of an earlier door or window. There is a fine Royal Arms of 1751 and a good holy water stoup by the south door with a carving of Tudor roses.

MINSTER IN SHEPPEY, *St Mary and St Sexburga*

The large, almost square, medieval gatehouse to the west of the church tells the visitor that here is no ordinary parish church. For nearly a thousand years this was both Minster Abbey and Minster parish church. Today it is one building, but formerly the present south aisle formed the parish church, while the north aisle belonged to the nuns. The parish church side has a distinct nineteenth-century feel to it, the result of a restoration of 1879 by Ewan Christian. It contains some old monuments; especially interesting is that to Sir Robert de Shurland (d. 1310) which is an effigy of a knight under a wall recess. Between the nuns' aisle and the parish church is the Cheyne tomb, commemorating Sir Thomas Cheyne (d. 1559). This imposing marble and alabaster table tomb shows him wearing the Order of the Garter. The north aisle – or nuns' church – has altogether more atmosphere with substantial remains of the original church built by Sexburga in AD 670. The arched heads of two Saxon windows survive in the southern wall, and the 'chancel' of the nuns' church has had its plaster removed to show the early rubble construction. It is separated from the rest of the church by a fine oak screen of about 1400. The whole church has a well-cared-for atmosphere and should be near the top of all visitors' lists.

MINSTER IN THANET, *St Mary the Virgin*

This Minster Abbey was founded in AD 669 by Domneva. The enormous parish church, built to the south-west of the abbey, dates from two separate periods. The nave is Norman, a magnificent piece of twelfth-century arcading with tall cylindrical pillars. The chancel is thirteenth century, with a three-light east window, each one double shafted inside. This end of the church has a simple stone vaulted ceiling which adds greatly to the grandeur. The glass is by Willement and dates from 1861. Ewan Christian restored the church in 1863 and added vaulted ceilings to the transepts. They had been intended by the medieval designers, but were never built. There is a set of eighteen fifteenth-century stalls with misericords and an excellent sixteenth-century font and cover.

MOLASH, *St Peter*

St Peter's is in a windswept location, in open farmland, with ancient yew trees and a patina of great antiquity. Abutting the north side of the tower, and entered from the church, is a rare medieval priest's house. The nave has a distinctly unusual atmosphere. It is lofty and plain, with much light flooding in from the large south windows. While there is no chancel arch there is a horizontal beam which carries the Royal Arms of George III. The three-crownpost roof is beautifully set off by whitewashed walls which are almost devoid of monuments. The chancel is something of an anti-climax, although there are traces of medieval wall paintings on the south wall.

MONKTON, St Mary Magdalene

A church of great charm that is smaller than it once was. In the north wall is a series of five blocked arches that formerly led into an aisle. The church is basically twelfth century, much remodelled a hundred years later. An unusual Norman piscina in the south-east corner is very low in the wall and shows the drastic raising of the floor that took place in the restoration of 1860. The wonderful altarpiece is Edwardian Pre-Raphaelite in design and above it is one small fragment of medieval glass. There are some medieval brasses, the finest, to John Spiller (d. 1460), is in the nave, while a palimpsest brass (inscribed on both sides) is fixed to the wall. The Jacobean pulpit has an hourglass stand for the preacher to time his sermon.

NACKINGTON, St Mary the Virgin

A Norman church with original windows in the nave, much remodelled in the thirteenth century when the little tower and south chapel were added. The crownpost roof in the nave may also date from this period. The church retains much good quality medieval glass for such a small building, but how it came to be here is something of a mystery. Experts say it belongs to the same studio as that in the seated figure of St Thomas à Becket – one of the few near-contemporary representations of the saint. He is wearing a blue chasuble and a green mitre, and is flanked on either side by two kings, Henry II (who is identified as such) and Louis VII of France. In the south chapel is a good double piscina and faint traces of medieval wall paintings.

NETTLESTEAD, St Mary the Virgin

The church is in a lovely setting next to Nettlestead Place, the former home of the Pympe family. In 1438 John Pympe demolished the old church and built from new on the remaining foundations. The only thing to survive above ground from the old church is the thirteenth-century west tower. The 'new church' built by Pympe is dignified by its six Perpendicular windows in the nave, which together form almost a wall of glass. They were originally filled with pictures of the twelve Apostles and armorial glass, but much was destroyed in an eighteenth-century storm, and what survived was restored in the early part of the twentieth century by Ward and Hughes. It was so well done that it is almost impossible for the casual visitor to say which is original and which is new. As a general rule of thumb the tracery panels at Nettlestead contain mainly medieval glass, while the majority of large lights show Ward and Hughes' work.

NEWCHURCH, Sts Peter and Paul

Not one of the most memorable churches on the Marsh, but still beautiful in its over-restored state. The church today dates from the thirteenth and fourteenth centuries, but its name implies that there was an earlier building here. The interior is more pleasing than the exterior, the finest single feature being the octagonal font which dates from the fifteenth century and incorporates the roses of Lancaster and York and the symbols of the patron saints, Sts Peter and Paul. Both chapels have medieval screens and there are well-defined rood loft openings. The ogee-headed piscina in the south chapel and the aumbry are typical of the fourteenth century. It is a pity that the nineteenth-century tiles are such a visual intrusion. The arcades of the nave should be contrasted with the thirteenth-century cut-through arches between chancel and chapels. The west tower – not tall as fourteenth-century structures go because of the marshy ground – leans to the west and is heavily buttressed. The shrinkage of the peat following drainage of the marshes for sheep grazing was to blame.

NEWENDEN, St Peter

An eye-catching tower and spire by G.M. Hills (architect of St Michael's, Tenterden), built in 1859, make a very plain fragment of a much larger medieval church pleasing to the eye. The original west tower and chancel were demolished in the seventeenth century because of their instability. The congregation struggled on with what was left until 1930 when a new chancel was built in the Romanesque style to the designs of Captain Shore of Northiam. It shows just how accomplished local architects who have a real sensitivity for old buildings can be. The contents of the church – pulpit of 1639, Royal Arms of George IV and modern altar rails – are all

NEWENDEN. The excellent chancel which was added to the remains of a medieval building in 1930.

overshadowed by the famous twelfth-century font. It has excellent crisp carvings of beasts including a wyvern and lion, but if its sculptor had some grand plan then it has been lost to twentieth-century eyes, for the designs on each side of the font have no apparent relationship to each other.

NEWINGTON, St Nicholas

Too close to the Channel Tunnel for comfort, this picturesque church dates from the twelfth century, and displays a good plain chancel arch. The north aisle is an addition of the thirteenth or fourteenth century. From the outside its cat-slide roof and the eccentric cupola on the tower create an artist's delight. Inside there are several curiosities – a series of three aumbries behind the high altar, a sixteenth-century pulpit made from parts of the former rood screen and a hagioscope from north chapel to chancel. The underfloor heating, similar to the Roman hypocaust systems, still survives, but is no longer in use. It is one of the few medieval heating systems to survive in England! On the south wall of the nave are a set of medieval brasses removed from the floor and a good collection of marble tablets to the Brockman and Drake-Brockman families, including one signed by Bacon in 1799.

NEWNHAM, Sts Peter and Paul

A most unusual and welcoming church consisting of tower, aisled nave, chancel and north and south chapels. There is no stained glass and the pews are plain, making the interior rather austere. The building dates from the thirteenth and fourteenth centuries – the double piscina in the chancel with an aumbry and image niche being the only medieval furnishings to survive. To the east of the narrow south aisle is the Champion Court Chapel, which was added to the church in the fifteenth century by the Champion family. In a church so thoroughly restored by the Victorians it is interesting to see this part of the building. Because it was privately owned the floor is uneven and unrestored. Two rustic little tablets in the floor date from the late seventeenth-century burial of Henry Cromys. The beautifully kept churchyard and the spiky 1860s exterior of the church add much to the character of the whole village.

NEW ROMNEY, St Nicholas

A wonderful church of grand proportions, the exterior of which is best seen from the east where the three reticulated windows of the Decorated period may be clearly seen. The nave is Norman, with interesting decoration on the arcades and solid circular piers. The church was owned by Potigny Abbey and in the thirteenth and fourteenth centuries it invested heavily in rebuilding the east end, with fine octagonal pillars, piscinae and sedilia in each of the three eastern chapels. Between the chancel and chapels are hagioscope openings. It is interesting that the floor remains unrestored, with brick, tile and old ledger slabs. This is the result of the intervention of the Society for the Protection of Ancient Buildings when John Oldrid Scott was over-restoring the church in 1878. The early aisles must have been very low as the Norman clerestory windows rise straight from the top of the arcade. The best place to see Norman work at New Romney is in the main west door where the zigzag decoration has few parallels in the county.

NORTHBOURNE, St Augustine

One of the few cruciform churches to have been built in Kent in the twelfth century, on the site of, and incorporating fragments of, a Saxon building. Curtains help shut off parts of the church during the winter months. There is a good mass dial by the main door. The Lady Chapel contains the monument to Sir Edwin Sandys and his wife (d. 1629). It is one of the best of its date in Kent and shows the pair in recumbent position hand in hand. Surprisingly the wordy inscription was not added until 1830! The chancel was refitted in the mid-nineteenth century but the east window shows good quality medieval stonework of thirteenth-century date.

NORTH CRAY, St James

Set away from a dual carriageway, the spire announces a church of the nineteenth century, built on the foundations of an earlier construction. It contains some good monuments – Lady Ellenborough (d. 1819) by Chantrey, Elizabeth Buggin (d. 1659) and William Wiffin (d. 1636). The unusual cast-iron Royal Arms in the north aisle are from the reign of James II and dated 1687. The most famous furnishings, however, are the continental wood carvings in the chancel, the majority of which were given to the church by Canon Johnston, vicar in the late nineteenth century. The reredos represents the Flight into Egypt and is in the style of Durer. The choir stalls have carvings of the Seven Acts of Mercy and the Nativity and include some nice traceried panels. Most of the woodwork is fifteenth and sixteenth century in date.

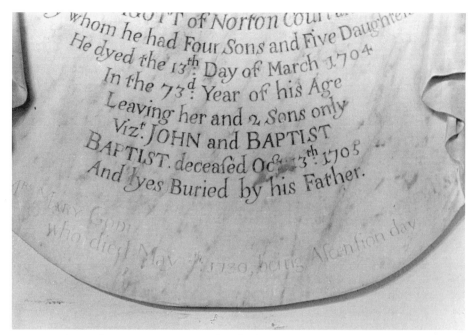

NORTON. An earlier monument to another family was re-used by a local stonemason to commemorate Mary Godi, who died in 1730.

NORTON, St Mary

The nave and chancel of this isolated church are of equal length, providing a most unusual aspect when viewed from the east end, with their lovely roof timbers exposed. The church is rather dark, partly due to the close proximity of the surrounding trees and partly due to the poor quality stained glass. However, it is the monuments which are so appealing, nearly all of them to families who lived at Norton Court. The most eye-catching is to Benjamin Godfrey (d. 1704). The top of his monument was later utilized as a memorial to the Revd W. Lushington (d. 1842). This was not the first re-use of a Godfrey tomb, for in 1730 the name of Mrs Mary Godi was inscribed on an existing memorial nearby!

NURSTEAD, St Mildred

One of the few churches dedicated to a Kentish saint – who was born at Minster in the seventh century. The church is a simple, late medieval structure of nave, chancel and west tower and stands in a large well-kept churchyard. Despite an over-heavy restoration the building retains much character. There is a good window between the ringing stage of the tower and the body of the church, to assist the medieval sanctus bell-ringer. Near the south door are the remains of a fifteenth-century holy water stoup, while the good ledger slabs in the chancel include one where a prominent mistake by the stonemason was corrected to the best of his ability!

OLD ROMNEY, St Clement

One of the most-visited Marsh churches, built on an artificial mound to protect it from the floodwaters. There is a Norman nave enlarged by the addition of aisles in the thirteenth century. Because of its virtually unrestored state it has many items of interest, the uneven floor creating a great atmosphere. The two hagioscopes to either side of the chancel arch are unusually large and little more than holes knocked into the wall. The rood loft staircase discovered in the 1920s still has its medieval door-frame – a rare survival indeed. In the north chapel is the mensa of the medieval altar. The delightful altar rails are early eighteenth century and present a run of very close-set balusters. The box pews and gallery are of later eighteenth-century date and were repainted for the Rank film, *Dr Syn*. The large Royal Arms of George III are dated 1800 – the lion has a very smug expression! An interesting and unusual sight is the font, the capitals of which are carved with different figures. They date from the fourteenth century, and are much worn, but with patience one can still pick out details of the grotesque animals.

OTFORD, St Bartholomew

This is a very wide church and relatively short, the walls being entirely rendered and a sombre grey in colour. From the roof hang a dozen brass chandeliers which create an impression of a warm country kitchen. At the west end above the tower door hang many hatchments, from a distance almost looking like a chessboard in their regularity. The pews are unusual too, for although they are of normal proportions they each have a little closing door. Through the wide chancel arch the east window shows some small seventeenth-century glass panels, rather unhappily set together, while below it is an interesting tomb constructed as an Easter Sepulchre. What a pity we do not know whose tomb it is. This is unusual as it is of late date, but still carries no identifying inscription.

OTFORD. This plain fifteenth-century canopied wall monument stands to the north of the altar and served as an Easter Sepulchre.

OTHAM, St Nicholas

The tower of Otham church is in an unusual position – in the south-east corner of the nave. In fact the church is altogether an unusual shape with a nave and chancel of equal length, both cells having a north chapel. The nave is Norman in date, as evidenced by the herringbone stonework between the porch and tower. There is a good holy water stoup near the south door while a piscina in the nave indicates the position of a medieval altar. The nave boasts an excellent crownpost roof, but that in the chancel was replaced in the nineteenth century. The strange font is fourteenth century and has four amusing carvings of two calves' heads, a face and a leaf. There are also several good monuments including one by Maximillian Colt which commemorates Levyn Buffkyn (d. 1620). It shows Mr and Mrs Buffkyn in bust form set within an interesting hanging marble surround.

PADDLESWORTH, St Benedict

Another two-cell church built of flint rubble. Of mid-Norman date it served a manor house and adjoining agricultural settlement which declined in the mid-seventeenth century when the lord of the manor moved elsewhere. Some windows were replaced in the thirteenth century when the present chancel arch with its funny faces was constructed. The aumbry in the south wall of the nave is formed of chalk blocks which are visible outside. At the back of the church is a fine medieval wooden screen brought from elsewhere and formed into a gallery. For much of its history this church was used as a barn and a cottage, and it is now cared for by the Churches Conservation Trust.

PADDLESWORTH, *St Oswald*

A two-cell Norman church with a good high chancel arch with typical cushion capitals. The church was much restored in the nineteenth century. A small aumbry, thirteenth-century piscina and a good nineteenth-century altar add much to our enjoyment of this isolated building. A small hagioscope leads from the south-east corner of the nave into the chancel, indicating the former position of a side altar.

PATRIXBOURNE, *St Mary*

A charming village church with a greater number of interesting furnishings than is usual in this part of the county. There are twelfth-century window openings in the chancel, while a lavish south doorway tells of an extremely wealthy medieval church. Next to it are the remains of eight mass dials – which must be a record! Inside, the south, or Bifrons, chapel is separated from the aisle by a screen and steps and there is a plain hagioscope to the chancel. Many mural tablets catch the eye and tell of the long association with the village of the Conyngham family. However, it is the stained glass which really deserves attention at Patrixbourne. Set among very basic nineteenth-century glass are many panels of seventeenth-century Swiss origin, including scenes of the Garden of Gethsemane, St Elizabeth of Hungary and the Raising of Lazarus. With the exception of Temple Ewell this is the largest collection of pictorial Swiss glass in a Kent church. By way of contrast, the north aisle displays an excellent twentieth-century window by G.C. Abbs.

PEMBURY, *St Peter (old church)*

A much restored Norman church, with a tiny twelfth-century window set just above the (later) porch roof. There is a good fifteenth-century low side window in the south-west corner of the chancel. The pews, pulpit and tiles are typical of mid-nineteenth century restorations, yet above is the fine nave roof of the usual crownpost type. It displays nicely pierced spandrels with a quatrefoil and dagger design. In 1846 Lord Camden built a new church on the main road in the village centre. Even so the old church is extremely well maintained and much loved in the neighbourhood. The churchyard contains many good headstones including one to Sir Morton Peto, the famous nineteenth-century engineer.

PENSHURST, St John the Baptist

A large sandstone church of nave, aisles, chancel and chapels that was restored by Scott in 1864. It stands in an excellent position set back from the street in a large well-kept churchyard. The tower is of three stages with four strange pinnacles set well back from the corners. Inside it is obvious that there have been many rebuildings and repairs, leaving a character of the Victorian period. The good chancel screen is by Bodley and Garner and dates from 1897. While it is well carved the design is more suited to a West Country church than to the Garden of England. The fifteenth-century font has been painted in bold colours in a way that can never have been imagined when it was new! Nearby is the Becket window designed by Lawrence Lee in 1970. It is quite unlike any other window in Kent and has an emphasis on heraldry – the figure of Becket and three knights are almost lost in the patchwork effect. Under the tower is the famous Albigensian Cross, a portion of thirteenth-century coffin lid with the effigy of a woman at prayer. The south chapel, which belongs to Penshurst Place, was rebuilt by Rebecca in 1820 and has a lovely painted ceiling. It contains some fine monuments including Sir Stephen de Pencester, a damaged thirteenth-century knight. Nearby is the large standing monument to the 4th Earl of Leicester (d. 1704) designed by William Stanton. It is a large urn flanked by two angels, above which are the earl's children's heads floating in the clouds!

PLAXTOL, No Dedication

Although there is no record of a medieval church here, the present building which dates from 1649 may stand on an early site. It is unusual to find a church of the Commonwealth period and for this reason it does not have a dedication. Although the basic hall church remains much rebuilding took place in the nineteenth century, giving the building a strangely urban feel. This is not helped by the fact that it is constructed of regular ragstone blocks which are galletted. The interior is now much lighter than the Victorians left it as war damage has removed most of the stained glass. The main feature of the interior is the hammerbeam roof, painted blue and more practical than decorative, and there is also some foreign wood carving incorporated in the reredos and pulpit.

PLUCKLEY, St Nicholas

A very pretty church of thirteenth- and fourteenth-century date. At the east end of the south aisle is the Dering chapel built in 1475 and separated from the church by two delightful screens – one contemporary with its construction, the other, nicely gilded, of 1635. There is an excellent crownpost roof in the nave and two modern stained glass windows. The east window represents Our Lord and the north window the Annunciation. They were designed by Francis Stephens and John Hayward in 1954. There is much emphasis in them on local objects, with oast houses and even Pluckley church clearly visible. In the nave are some brasses to members of the Dering family – all made in the 1630s by Sir Edward Dering in order to show his family ancestry! They bear dates from the fifteenth and sixteenth centuries and could easily mislead those without specialist knowledge.

PRESTON NEXT WINGHAM, St Mildred

The church stands in a delightful setting on a small rise opposite the 'big house' with its two large lakes. The path leads up to the north door from which we can see that the church was much altered in the nineteenth century, the most notable features of that period being the dormer windows. Inside they are rather strange and when viewed from the west end resemble a flight of Concordes! When they were added the windows in the two aisles were blocked, which makes the church decidedly dark. In the nave is the most unusual feature – Dr Bray's parochial library, one of eighty or so bookcases given to poor churches by the founder of the SPCK. It has iron handles on either side, but the heavy leather books it contained would not have made transportation easy!

QUEENBOROUGH, Holy Trinity

The town of Queenborough grew to serve the long-vanished castle which had been founded in the fourteenth century by Edward III. The church – which should not be missed – dates from 1366 and consists of nave, chancel, west tower and south porch. Its churchyard is entirely crowded with headstones to those associated with the Royal Dockyard at Sheerness. Inside the church are two main items of interest. The most striking is the nave roof which is ceiled and painted with looming clouds. This work dates from the seventeenth century, as does the other item of note: the font. This is dated 1610 and includes a fine carved picture of Queenborough Castle, with four corner turrets and two cannon halfway up the walls. The fine Royal Arms are of Queen Anne's reign – the lion has the head of Charles I – and show the loyalty of the people of Queenborough to the monarch who had granted them their town charter.

RAINHAM, St Margaret

A large and interesting church that is hard to miss – the enormous tower is about a hundred feet high and looms over the High Street. Although the church is Norman there is little visible work earlier than the thirteenth century. There is an aisled nave, chancel and north chapel. At the east end of the nave (there is no chancel arch) the ceiling is boarded to form a celure, or canopy of honour over the rood, painted with the sun in splendour, the symbol of King Edward IV. After the Wars of the Roses each sun had a Tudor rose inserted into it for good measure! On the south side of the chancel is a small length of decorative arcading of thirteenth-century date with one original lancet window remaining. Below this are three stepped sedilia and a pretty piscina. Between the high altar and north chapel is a large sixteenth-century chest tomb with panelled sides and a brass indent, while in the chapel itself is a series of monuments to the Tufton family, including two large marble statues. These commemorate the 2nd Earl of Thanet (d. 1670) and the 3rd Earl who died in 1679. The east window of the chapel shows the four parables and was designed as a thank offering after the Second World War by Francis Spear. The lovely church chest has a nine-bay arcade incised into it, showing decorated tracery, and dates therefore from the beginning of the fourteenth century.

RAMSGATE, St George

Built in 1824 to the designs of Henry Hemsley, St George's is a Commissioners Church, partly financed by Parliament. The enormous west tower, with lantern turret, is by far the most imposing landmark in the town. Like most churches of its date there is a 'public hall' feel to the interior, with minimal Gothic detailing and use of cast-iron columns. The altar stands in a small eastern apse with a pretty ceiling and the pulpit stands exceptionally high, with a view over the pews which were installed in 1844. In the west gallery is a rather stolid piece of Victorian painting – *From Darkness to Light* – showing three angels carrying a saint to heaven. It was painted in 1885 by Henry Weigall. In the Lady Chapel is the Dunkirk window, designed by A.E. Buss in 1961. It is of two lights and shows the Dunkirk beaches, Ramsgate harbour and other local scenes, together with the emblems of all the organizations that played a part in the evacuation. It is of greater historical interest than artistic merit!

RODMERSHAM, St Nicholas

A good example of a village church surrounded by orchards. The building consists of nave and chancel with south aisle and chapel. The west tower is exceptionally tall and proud. In the north wall of the nave are excellent examples of rood loft stairways, the top of each doorway having shouldered arches. The most interesting parts of the church are the chancel and chapel. The former contains an excellent altar by Buckeridge and Hoyce (1888) and an east window of German glass by Bayer of Munich, dated 1881. On the south side is the excellent fifteenth-century *wooden* sedilia of three canopied seats – almost unique in England. It backs on to a contemporary parclose screen that divides the chancel from south chapel. The chapel contains two panels of blind Norman arcading and a good east window by Ward and Hughes. In the south aisle is a blocked low side window that could have served a side altar.

ROLVENDEN, St Mary the Virgin

Standing high on a rise to the south of the village street, this is a prominent sandstone building of thirteenth- and fourteenth-century date. The most interesting feature is the family pew built by the owners of Hole Park in the eighteenth century. It stands on a gallery and comes complete with tables and chairs! The screen beneath it was added by W.D. Caroe in the 1920s. In the arch to the opposite chapel is a memorial to Lt Tennant designed by Lutyens. There are three holy water stoups in the church and a very good piscina in the chancel. The font is of about the same date and shows the arms of two prominent medieval families, the Guilfords and the Culpepers. The church contains a seventeenth-century wooden alms box and on the south door-frame is a medieval mass dial.

RUCKINGE, St Mary Magdalene

A large church of Norman origins, the west door being a much-weathered example of twelfth-century work. The south doorway is also Norman and has the remains of two mass dials carved into the quoins. The stonework inside shows clear signs of fire damage, and a nice crownpost roof of the fourteenth century probably marks the date of the rebuilding after the fire. Of the same period are the returned stalls on the south side of the chancel – the fronts being little more than a series of plain upright planks, with some super poppyheads at each end. Outside, the upper stage of the tower is thirteenth century and has a small pyramidal roof with needle spire.

RYARSH, St Martin

An attractive church which stands a long way from its (later) village. The building is of Norman date. The north wall of the nave displays some good herringbone masonry and a tiny round-headed window above. Inside there is an unusual Norman pillar piscina on the south side of the chancel. A south aisle was added in the fifteenth century and has a nicely proportioned gabled east end. The rood loft staircase is still visible inside as are the responds of the eastern triplet of Norman windows, replaced by the present window in the Perpendicular period.

ST MARY IN THE MARSH, St Mary

A Norman church with a heavily buttressed west tower, aisles with separate roof structures and a generously proportioned chancel. The latter contains an excellent small sedilia and double piscina displaying super little carved faces. The Royal Arms are those of George III, and the opening for the rood loft may still be seen. There is no chancel arch – possibly due to a lack of suitable building stone on the Marsh. The narrow nature of the north aisle shows that it was built for processions rather than seating. In the churchyard is the grave of author E.M. Nesbit.

ST NICHOLAS AT WADE, St Nicholas

Its tall fourteenth-century tower dominates the flat farmland nearby. Over the font is a section of fourteenth-century roof – the lovely colours of the beams contrasting with the whitewashed walls, while next to the main door is a ladder leading up to a room over the porch which was used as a workshop by the local plumber in the eighteenth century! To the south of the chancel arch is a good pulpit with the date 1615 prominently displayed. The chancel is raised only slightly from the nave and to the north is the Bridges chapel which contains some nice memorial tablets. But one must return to the font to see the most memorable piece of work: the remains of a stone vaulted ceiling filling the base of the tower. How grand it must have looked when new – but even today in its truncated form one can imagine its original appearance.

SANDHURST, St Nicholas

A large sturdy tower overlooks the valley dividing Kent and Sussex. It dates, as does much of the church, from the fourteenth century. The arcades are of dumpy octagonal pillars which have lancet clerestory windows set into the walls above. There are some notable fragments of medieval glass in the south aisle, together with an excellent modern etched glass window. The tower is flanked by the aisles (see also Wickhambreux). The north aisle displays the original entrance to the rood loft staircase. At the west end is a nice octagonal sandstone font with a series of decorated window designs enlivening its sides.

SANDWICH, St Clement

This is one of the most impressive churches in east Kent. The central tower is an elaborate Norman structure with a circular stair turret. Viewed from

SANDWICH, St Peter. This late thirteenth-century sedilia and piscina are so crisp in appearance that one suspects they are a nineteenth-century rebuild.

the west the three gables of the church present an unusual contrast: the outer aisles have tall pointed gables while the west wall of the nave has an almost flat gable. Internally the nave ceiling follows the same flat form, with little angels in its centre. Its predecessor must have been much lower, as indicated by the obvious roof line immediately above the crossing arch of the tower. The chancel is Early English and the east window is made up of a group of three lancets. There is a good Tudor hagioscope between chancel and north chapel, and the choir stalls are also of fifteenth-century date. The early fifteenth-century octagonal font has lost the statues from its corners, but shows the Tudor Rose, the Arms of the Cinque Ports and those of England and France.

SANDWICH, St Peter

Easily identified from afar by its unusual cupola built in the seventeenth century to complete the reconstruction of the tower following its total collapse. The base of the tower still displays some medieval stonework, whereas the top is seventeenth-century brick. Their interior is tall and light with a heavily timbered crownpost roof. Among many items of interest the church contains three fine canopied wall monuments. One of them shows a husband and wife of mid-fourteenth-century date. Their heads are turned a little to the south to face the altar and they have an animated lion at their feet. The church is now maintained by the Churches Conservation Trust who allow the nave to be used for a variety of alternative uses. The Trust also has charge of St Mary's church a little further down the road.

SEAL, Sts Peter and Paul

Quite a landmark from the M26, Seal church stands a little to the north of its village, on high ground, overlooking the Kemsing Valley. The visitor is struck by the length of the building, constructed in the thirteenth century and altered a hundred years later. The south arcade is medieval while the north is Victorian. The wonderful chancel screen was designed by C.R. Ashbee in 1931. Among other fine furnishings is the wooden lectern which shows the Angel of Victory supporting the bible. It is possible that the same (unknown) designer worked on the bronze memorial to Elizabeth Mills in the Lady Chapel. This shows the girl, who died aged six, asleep between two angel's wings. There are plenty of other memorials of note, including several wall tablets by Chantrey designed in the 1830s.

SELLING, St Mary the Virgin

Set on a hilltop among orchards, Selling has more in the way of furnishings of interest than most churches in the area. The east window has glass from about 1300 which shows St John, St Mary Magdalene, the Blessed Virgin Mary and St Margaret of Antioch. The figures are set into a grisaille pattern with heraldic shields below. These show the Arms of Edward I, Queen Eleanor of Castile and Queen Margaret of France. The glass may have been moved about in the nineteenth century, but it was so well done that the joins do not show. In the south chapel hang two flags flown at the Battle of Trafalgar in 1805. There are Royal Arms of Queen Victoria and several good nineteenth-century memorial tablets. The west window, which represents the Resurrection, was designed by Willement in 1850. He lived at nearby Faversham. A window in the north aisle by A.E. Buss (1970) shows the Benedicte and includes a picture of Selling church. Another window, by Powells, includes symbols of the Australian sugar industry!

SEVENOAKS, St Nicholas

The church looks well from the main street, with its east end almost on the road. Built of local stone, the nave, aisles, chapels and tower are typical of fifteenth-century design. The church has been so often restored – in 1812, 1878, 1954 and most recently in 1994 when a crypt was built – that its historical interest is limited. However, the stained glass windows by Kempe and Heaton, Butler and Bayne are of excellent quality, especially those in the south aisle. There are also some interesting monuments, including one to William Lambarde (d. 1601), the first Kentish historian.

SHOREHAM, Sts Peter and Paul

The porch is of very solid fifteenth-century workmanship with good, though weathered, carvings in the spandrels and plain bargeboards above. Inside the church the greatest treasure is the rood screen, with its original loft – 6 ft 6 in wide. It shows the Pomegranate of Catherine of Aragon carved on its door, and this may help us date it to the visit of Henry VIII and his queen to nearby Otford Palace in 1520. The pulpit of 1827 is by Blore and is one of two in the county that originally stood in Westminster Abbey (the other is at Trottiscliffe). In the south wall is a window of 1903 depicting Joy, Creation and Love by the firm of Morris and Co. At the west end is a picture of Lt Verney Cameron, who led the expedition to find David Livingstone in 1873, painted by Charles Cope RA.

SHORNE, Sts Peter and Paul

The church stands in the centre of a picturesque village. It is Saxon in origin, as indicated by the double splayed window over the north arcade, and contains several interesting features from various periods. An excellent effigy of Henry de Cobham (d. 1315) sits on a nineteenth-century plinth. He is shown as a cross-legged knight with his feet on a crouched leopard and his head on a helmet. Behind him stands a good fifteenth-century parclose screen while the rood screen has medieval work at its base and a late nineteenth-century top. There is an interesting fifteenth-century font with a variety of symbols including a smooth Agnus Dei sheep, possibly a medieval joke on the place name, Shorne.

SIBERTSWOLD, St Andrew

Sibertswold is sometimes shown on maps as Shepherdswell. The tiny church is entirely Victorian. It is a building of great charm which was designed by Benjamin Ferrey in 1863. It is built of local flint with Bath stone dressings and is distinguished by a little spirelet over, but not quite on, the west end. The interior is simple and consists of nave, apsidal chancel and little transepts. The east windows are by the St Helens Crown Glass Co., and represent the Ascension and Four Evangelists. The south window of 1900, by Kempe, shows the Epiphany. The good polished marble decorative shafts to either side of the chancel arch, together with the corbels in the nave, are typical of Ferrey's work. It is a pity that the original font, which was of fine Cornish marble and had matching marble shafts, had to be destroyed, owing to its instability, in 1955.

SMALLHYTHE, St John the Baptist

Built of brick in 1516 after a large fire destroyed the whole village, Smallhythe church is a simple rectangular box, rather taller than it need be, its height emphasized by the crow-stepped gables that rise in ten steps. The west wall has a little image niche under the gable. The interior is as plain as the exterior and has a wooden chancel screen and nicely tiled floor. Yet the church receives numerous visitors on the strength of its associations with Dame Ellen Terry, the famous actress, who lived at nearby Smallhythe Place. Without the fame of this former resident and the dedication of its congregation, this church might not have such an assured future.

SMARDEN, St Michael the Archangel

A large fourteenth-century church entered from the High Street by a path which runs under a cottage. The building is full of interesting objects including, on either side of the chancel arch, two tiers of blank arcades that each provided a reredos to side altars. They are quite a sight – their present appearance enhanced by early twentieth-century paintings. There is a really solid medieval almsbox of late fifteenth-century date. A copper plate was fixed to the top to form a slot for the coins – and uniquely this piece of copper was really Limoges enamel! The scenes may still be seen, even though it is badly worn. Under a south window in the chancel are three elaborate sedilia, with a nice battlemented top, and nearby there is a piscina, aumbry, low side window and even a wafer oven! There is a large recess in the north wall of the chancel that formed an Easter Sepulchre. In the south wall of the nave is the fifteenth-century rood loft staircase.

SNARGATE, St Dunstan

An over-restored church in a leafy position off the main road. Mainly thirteenth century in date, with a fifteenth-century west tower and eighteenth-century brick porch. There is a good square thirteenth-century font and remains of the rood loft staircase. By far the most interesting feature is the large wall painting of a ship opposite the main door. It seems to date from the sixteenth century and was only discovered in 1971 under a layer of whitewash. The tie-beams of the barrel-vaulted roof have a relief carving on the underside, almost forming a decorative boss – a very unusual feature so far from any centre of medieval craftsmanship.

SNAVE, St Augustine

A very simple church comprising nave, chancel and north chapel. Like many of the neighbouring churches it is beautifully whitewashed throughout, which enhances its simplicity. The encaustic tiles in the chancel, added by the Victorian restorers, are rather out of place, but the visitor would be advised to look up to appreciate the nave roof, where three sturdy tie-beams support three graceful crownposts. The best time to visit this atmospheric church is when the daffodils are in bloom and the lambs are appearing on the surrounding marshes.

SNODLAND, *All Saints*

In an awkward position, cut off from its village by the railway and somewhat compromised by the adjoining paper mill. The present church has been extended from its fourteenth century origins, most noticeably by the addition of a tall tower in the fifteenth century. There is a rood loft staircase in the south wall and on a pillar nearby can still be seen a nice fourteenth-century Crucifixion painted on the wall within an incised outline. The church was over-restored by Blomfield in 1870 and suffered damage in the Second World War when the medieval glass was destroyed. Fragments have been assembled where possible. New windows were installed, including the thirty-six symbols of the saints in the east window by Hugh Easton (1953), and the Becket Pilgrim window by Moira Forsyth (1966). A large memorial in the south aisle commemorates Thomas Waghorn (d. 1850), who pioneered the overland route to India.

SOUTHFLEET, *St Nicholas*

A large interesting church totally built in the fourteenth century of a flint and stone rubble mixture. The arcades of both north and south aisles are of the standard octagonal pattern. The font is very boldly carved on each of its faces; particularly interesting is the representation of a chalice with the wafer appearing as a sunburst. The five-light east window of 1854 is by O'Connor. In the south aisle is the table tomb of John Sedley (d. 1520) while his great-grandson John (d. 1603) is commemorated by a large standing wall monument. The chancel has a three-seater sedilia and some medieval stalls with simple misericords.

SPELDHURST, *St Mary the Virgin*

The outstanding feature of this solid Victorian church, built by John Oldrid Scott in 1871, is the series of windows by the firm of Morris and Co. The east window of the north aisle represents some early saints including Alban and Aidan, while that in the west end shows six angels. Nearby is an early representation of Kentish saints, whose popularity was increasing in the middle of the nineteenth century, including Augustine, Ethelbert and Bertha. The east window is by the same firm, but dates from after the death of Burne-Jones and is not so finely executed. The oak reredos was added by Charles Oldrid Scott in 1925, who also worked on the altar rails and low chancel screen. Outside is a good monument made of Coade artificial stone in 1807.

STAPLE, St James the Great

The greater part of this pretty church is fourteenth century, although parts of the walling of the tower are probably Saxon. The font is fifteenth century and has good relief carving of the Four Evangelists supported by a variety of wild men of the woods! The chancel displays a low side window of rare lancet design (there is a mass dial outside). The church tower has a one-handed clock with a IV instead of the more usual IIII. The church was restored by Street in 1868 and he created the pervading atmosphere noticeable today.

STAPLEHURST, All Saints

The south doorway is the feature most visitors seek out – the ironwork on it dates from about 1050 and is of Danish influence, showing the story of the Norse Day of Judgement. It is difficult to make out all the features that the design represents, but with perseverance a shoal of fish, a single large flying fish and an eel may be identified. There is a theory that it was made for somewhere more important than Staplehurst and that it found its way here at a later date. After the door the rest of the church is rather tame, consisting of nave, chancel, south aisle and chapel. To the north of the chancel stood an anchorite's cell – the small window that led to it may still be seen and the foundations are visible outside. The glass in the north window (1952) is by Owen Jennings. Under the tower is a series of colourful Tudor panels, four of which have shears carved on them, reminding us that Staplehurst was very much a part of the medieval wool trade, whose profits helped rebuild this church.

STOCKBURY, St Mary

A fire of 1836 and a restoration of 1851 have left their marks on this prominent Downland church. The east wall of the chancel contains three lancets, of nineteenth-century origin, which contain some lovely glass of the early years of the twentieth century. To the north and south of the chancel are transepts separated by nicely carved screens. The southern transept is the more picturesque, for its roof timbers are exposed and below, in its east wall, are three sturdy windows of which the centre one is blocked. The west end of the nave is built up to form a platform upon which stands the organ. On either side of the chancel arch are typical nineteenth-century Ten Commandment boards, with good marble shafting to mirror the medieval work in the chancel.

STODMARSH, St Mary

The church stands intimately on a right-hand bend of the road. It is an extremely simple building of solid twelfth- and thirteenth-century construction. The chancel was rebuilt during the latter period. There is a small south porch which shields a doorway on which are carved many so-called Crusaders' Crosses. Like most churches in east Kent Stodmarsh was restored in the 1880s and the roofs of both nave and chancel show this to unfortunate effect. Apart from that the church is a delight. There is a plain rood screen on a stone base which is well set off against the cream washed walls of the chancel. At the west end the bell turret is supported internally by a huge X-shaped brace, which is a unique feature in Kent, and far more functional than pretty.

STONE, St Mary the Virgin

An impressive church in a depressing location, on the very edge of an old chalk quarry. The lavish thirteenth-century work was not completed at the time, and was only finished by Street who carried out a scholarly restoration in 1859. There is much emphasis on Purbeck marble shafting and carved stonework, especially in the chancel where the twenty spandrels of the wall arcading are covered in decorative work. One of the designs is of a lizard (with a handsome row of teeth) eating a leaf. The chancel is vaulted in stone, the result of Street's restoration. The pulpit was carved by Earp (1860) and the east window, of the same date, is by Wailes. There is an excellent brass to John Lambarde, Rector (d. 1408), showing him in his vestments. A later hanging monument to George Sharp (d. 1810) is by R. Watson, a local stonemason from Dartford.

STURRY, St Nicholas

A church that is often overlooked by visitors who are drawn to nearby Canterbury. As a possession of St Augustine's Abbey in the Middle Ages, it is easy to see the amount of money lavished on this church over the centuries. This is nowhere more apparent than in the fourteenth-century work when the aisles were added to a twelfth-century nave. The extremities of the building – tower and chancel – are both still Norman and show ample architectural evidence in the form of round-headed windows. The chancel has an aumbry and early thirteenth-century piscina. There are few old monuments because of a severe nineteenth-century restoration, but there is a small fifteenth-

STONE. The pulpit designed by Street in 1860 and carved by Earp, who also carved the font at Rochester Cathedral.

century inscription near the font. The porch is a fine sixteenth-century timber-framed structure with later brick infilling.

SUTTON AT HONE, St John the Baptist

A fascinating church showing good quality medieval work and contrasting nineteenth-century rebuilding. The main chancel and nave date from the fourteenth century – a period of much rebuilding in this part of Kent – while the south aisle is separated from the nave by an unequivocally Victorian arcade. In April 1615 the church was accidentally burnt down by a man shooting pigeons (see also Charing) and all the furnishings date from after this period. Especially fine is the early seventeenth-century pulpit. The monument in the south aisle to Sir Thomas Smythe (d. 1625), an early official of the East India Company, is a good example of alabaster craftsmanship.

SWINGFIELD, St Peter

This church is built in flint and rubble construction and the west tower has a remarkably wide stair turret. As one enters through the south porch one can see the remains of two mass dials made redundant by the construction of the porch itself. By the pulpit is a most unusual feature – the south-east window of the nave has had its sill cut away to provide space for a wooden ladder to give access to the rood loft. This window now contains a lovely stained glass representation of the Crucifixion with a charming little sun and moon at the top. At Swingfield the nineteenth-century north aisle detracts from the thirteenth-century nave; its scale, materials and lumpy effect do nothing to complement this charming church.

TEMPLE EWELL, Sts Peter and Paul

In a strange position, oddly isolated from the main road and pretty valley below. The church is a bare structure of Norman origin, over-restored in 1870 by Talbot Bury, whose work in Bath stone can only be described as unfortunate. The east window is by Martin Travers – Comper's pupil – but is not a good example of his work. However, there are some good examples of Swiss glass comparable to the windows at Patrixbourne. Probably the finest is the Flight into Egypt. One only wishes for more splashes of colour to enliven this otherwise plain church.

TENTERDEN, St Mildred

A superb church, which despite a heavy-handed restoration by G.M. Hills in 1864 still has much of interest. The nave ceiling is exceptional fifteenth-century work, rather more domestic in feel than is normal in an ecclesiastical building. There are two blocked thirteenth-century windows above the chancel arch – an unusual position for Kent. The five bay aisles are extremely narrow. The south aisle windows by Hughes of 1865 are rather fun. In the north chapel is a fine alabaster standing monument to Herbert Whitfield (d. 1622) and his wife. This monument cuts off the base of the north-east window and has many colourful coats of arms. The chancel screen and pulpit are late nineteenth century and fit in with the medieval architecture better than most of their period.

TEYNHAM, St Mary

An enormous building in an isolated position overlooking farmland. The church is entered under a tower built in the fourteenth century, which completed a westward rebuilding of a thirteenth-century church that boasted very large transepts. The Victorian east window (for which there is a design hanging on the wall) was destroyed in the Second World War and replaced by the present glass to the designs of Hugh Easton. In the north transept are some fragments of fifteenth-century glass. The pulpit is Jacobean. In the south transept are some excellent brasses including one to John Frogenhall (d. 1444), showing him wearing the SS-pattern collar of the Lancastrian cause.

THURNHAM, St Mary

A charming, if somewhat plain, church set just off the Pilgrims' Way. In the north wall of the nave is a blocked Norman window, while the north chapel may be entered under an arch of possibly twelfth-century origin. For much of its history this chapel was the private pew of the Sheldon family. The nave runs straight into the chancel which is distinguished by a graceful east window of four lights capped with three circles of tracery. Below the window there is much panelling given in the early part of the twentieth-century and a small single sedile, piscina and aumbry of thirteenth-century date.

TROTTISCLIFFE. The eighteenth-century altar rail which shows, just left of centre, the unique moneybox that 'churched' women would have used to donate their thank-offering.

TROTTISCLIFFE, Sts Peter and Paul

Tucked away by farm buildings well away from the village, this is one of the most rewarding churches in west Kent. Although it is a simple rectangular building with an added south tower it is full of character and furnishings of quality. The pulpit came from Westminster Abbey in 1820 and completely dominates the interior. It was designed by Henry Keene in the late 1700s and was thrown out to make room for the coronation of George IV. The sounding board is carried up like a palm tree. The altar rails are eighteenth century and just to the left of the main gate is a most unusual feature, an offertory box for the churching of women. There is a good selection of stained glass for such a small church – ranging from large fifteenth-century canopy work in the tracery of the north window, through Ward and Hughes' glass of 1885 in the west window, to Comper-style glass in the south wall and a new window by Keith and Judy Hill of Bishop Gundulf (who lived in the neighbouring manor house in the eleventh century).

TUDELEY, All Saints

Set in a farmyard, this church draws thousands of visitors to see the only complete set of stained glass by Marc Chagall in England. The earliest glass is that in the east window which was installed as a memorial to Sarah d'Avigdor Goldsmid in 1967. She died in a sailing accident and is shown floating in the waves. After its erection a whole set of glass was designed and made for the church, although it was not fully installed in the church until after Chagall's death. The Victorian glass which had to be removed to accommodate it has been placed in light boxes below the tower, which is entered below the super organ which was built in 1994. The entire church is light and open, with high quality ceiling, pews and floor. It is an example to all that twentieth-century workmanship – providing it is of good quality – can enhance any medieval building.

TUNBRIDGE WELLS, King Charles the Martyr

The red brick church stands on a busy junction at the end of the Pantiles whose patrons it was built to serve in 1678. Within thirty years it had been extended on two occasions and more or less reached its present size. The ceiling is dated 1678 and is rather domestic in character, based on deep circular domes with putti, palms and swags. The stained glass in the east window is based on a picture by Alex Ender and was designed by Heaton, Butler and Bayne in 1901. There is an excellent window under the north gallery designed by Lawrence Lee in 1969. The church was sympathetically restored by Ewan Christian in 1882, when the little chancel was added. The woodwork in the chancel was brought from one of Wren's City of London churches. Outside the west wall of the church, set into the footpath, is a boundary marker to show the former parish boundaries of Tonbridge and Speldhurst.

TUNSTALL, St John the Baptist

The west doorway, with an ogee-headed arch, is fourteenth century in date. It has many crockets running up the entire structure, although the finial has been lost and the string course that originally followed its outline now covers just a small piece of blank wall. The south doorway has two unusual grated ventilation openings (see also Hawkinge). The nave is dignified by a hanging rood designed by Martin Travers in 1967 and may be seen against the elaborate east window of 1850, the glass of which was designed by Ward and

Hughes. The south chapel, which is built of flint, was enlarged in brick in 1655 and contains some interesting monuments, most impressive of which is that to Sir Edward Hales (d. 1654). Sir Edward lies on his left side with big chubby cheeks. It is a very late date for a figure to be shown wearing plate armour.

ULCOMBE, All Saints

A lovely church, full of atmosphere. There is much plain glass which makes a light interior. In the south aisle there are a surprising number of medieval wall paintings, especially fine being those of St Michael and the Crucifixion. In the sanctuary, on the north wall, is a superb drawing – which was never painted – showing five priests. The south chapel has a good set of decorated windows with reticulated tracery. There are several image brackets. The north chapel contains some excellent monuments, including three plain tomb chests, one of which commemorates William Maydeston (d. 1419). The arch from the north chapel to the nave has on its underside some thirteenth-

ULCOMBE. One of the excellent wall paintings of the thirteenth century which shows St Michael on the left and the Devil on the right.

century chevron painting and an entrance to the rood loft stairway. In the chancel are some good stalls with five misericords, showing two dragons and a lion-like creature.

UNDERRIVER, St Margaret

One of the smaller churches of Sir G.G. Scott, built in 1870 and paid for by the Hon. John Davison MP, at a cost of £2,500. It is a plain and simple building of nave and chancel, constructed of local sandstone in thirteenth-century style. The enjoyable fittings are mostly of later date, nearly all added by a vicar in the early years of the twentieth century. Outside, the church is distinguished by an excellent lychgate and a pretty west gable under which is a large clock face.

UPCHURCH, St Mary the Virgin

Sir Francis Drake's father was vicar here in the sixteenth century. The church is memorable for its odd spire, a little like that at Bexley. It is four-sided to start with and suddenly changes into an octagon a third of the way up. There seems to be no structural reason for this change. Inside the church there is much work of the thirteenth century including three sedilia which, unusually, stand below the arch to the south chapel. The arch is finished by a very crisply carved head (possibly too crisp – it may result from Butterfield's restoration of the church in 1885). Behind the sedilia, separating the seats from the chapel, is a charming wooden screen, with nine tall ogee-headed arches and a panel of pierced trefoils and quatrefoils. Both north and south chapels contain fragments of medieval glass while in the north chapel you may find a collection of medieval tiles, including one that shows a hunched figure with a staff and hat – possibly representing a pilgrim. This is a particularly rewarding church that stands in a little-visited part of the county.

WALDERSHARE, All Saints

The church stands within the grounds of Waldershare Park and is not easy to find. Through a lychgate, in a tree-shaded churchyard, the three eastern gables may be seen. The centre one is of natural flint, whereas the outer two are of brickwork, and these sum up the charm of this church – one of contrasts. The nave was almost rebuilt in the nineteenth century and you could almost imagine it belonging to a suburban church of the

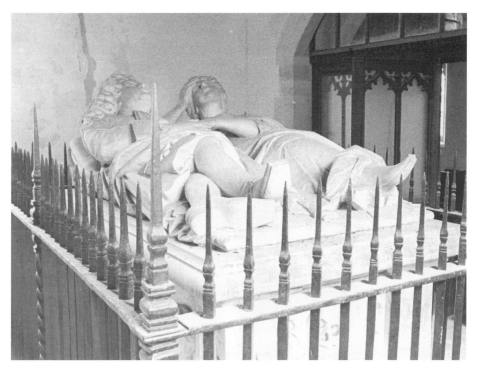

WALDERSHARE. The south chapel contains this excellent seventeenth-century effigy of Susan Bertie and her husband, set within its original iron railings.

1870s. The roof is high, the walls are bare and the character rather austere. The chancel, too, has a Victorian feel with a heavy marble reredos and stencilled walls. Leading off north and south of the chancel are the brick chapels which we noted on the outside. The south chapel is the earlier, dating from 1697, and contains the tomb chest of Susan Bertie. The same tomb also commemorates Montague, Earl of Lindsey, who was loyal to Charles I, and is noted as 'having attended his sacred Majestie to his grave and giving him a Christian burial at Windsor after his barbarous and horrid murder'. The north chapel was built in 1712 to accommodate the monument to Sir Henry Furness who built the present mansion house in the park. This monument only just fits into its chapel and rises in stages like a wedding cake, with four life-sized broken-hearted ladies at the base for starters. As a conversation piece it is unrivalled in a country church. The church is no longer used and is maintained as a private chapel by the Earl of Guilford.

WALTHAM, St Bartholomew

More interesting than beautiful, the church consists of nave, chancel and central tower. The nave is twelfth century – a north window still dates from this period. In the thirteenth-century chancel are the outstanding sedilia, probably erected to mark the completion of the rebuilding works at that end of the church. Its shafts are of Bethersden marble and the top is boldly embattled. The church boasts a fine Royal Arms of George III. The corbels that supported the rood beam may still be seen while at the opposite end of the building is a charming eighteenth-century gallery built for musicians. Outside, on the south wall, are the remains of two mass dials.

WAREHORNE, St Matthew

Almost a 'Marsh' church in feel, although it stands on high ground with distant views of the levels below. The church is entered through a nice eighteenth-century brick porch with a Dutch gable. The font is seventeenth century and carved from local stone, but it stands on a quite inappropriate

WAREHORNE. Like many churches in the area there is no chancel arch. The tie-beams of the roof have had to be extended to take account of outward settlement. The box pews are nineteenth century.

Victorian base. Nearby, on a pedimented screen at the base of the tower, is a good Royal Arms of Queen Anne. The church is light and airy and the 'empty' chancel greatly enhances our appreciation of the interior. The plain box pews are of early nineteenth-century date and there are text and commandment boards throughout. The sedilia were formed by dropping the window-sill and slotting a tiny piscina into the easternmost end. The arcades are formed of circular pillars of Bethersden marble that are curiously stratified, while the upper doorway for the rood loft is plainly seen at the north-east corner of the nave. Its walkway must have inconveniently crossed the east window of the north aisle as its staircase is in the north aisle wall.

WESTERHAM, St Mary the Virgin

The tower staircase is the feature most visitors remember, a wide circular construction of timber enclosed within vertical posts. It is quite an eye-catcher and has stood here for nearly five hundred years. The church has something of a Victorian feel to it by virtue of the thorough restoration and enormous amounts of money lavished on it at that time. Yet there are earlier features of note – most importantly the Royal Arms of Edward VI. They are painted on a wooden board, not stretched canvas, and the supporters – which include a dragon (unicorns didn't come along until 1603) – are very tall and lean. In fact the lion is little more than a pussy cat with his crown at quite a jaunty angle! There are some very fine sixteenth-century memorial brasses, and a consecration cross may be picked out at the base of the tower. The south chapel has a fourteenth-century piscina with a credence shelf. However, when it comes to furnishings it is the stained glass that impresses. The east window is by Holiday (1882), the south chapel east window Crucifixion by Kempe (1888) is particularly good, while a north aisle window is by Morris and Co. to the designs of Burne-Jones and dates from 1909.

WEST FARLEIGH, All Saints

In a charming position on the south slope of the narrow Medway Valley, this church is a very early Norman survivor. The east window is made up of a set of three single lights, the central one being original Norman work, the other two having Early English lancets which replaced the Norman openings. The amazing chancel arch is constructed entirely of tufa, and is one of the best tufa constructions in south-east England. To the south is a thirteenth-century piscina that served a side altar. There is a large Royal Arms of George III on the west wall.

WEST KINGSDOWN, St Edmund

Very much the 'church in the woods', St Edmund's takes a bit of finding. It is a typical building of the Saxo-Norman overlap, with the corners formed, unusually, of flint. The tower originally had an eastern apse like the one that still exists at Godmersham, and its blocked-up arch may be clearly seen. There was a south aisle too, the arcade of which is also blocked, and whose roofline can be found on the west wall of the tower. The church contains one of the finest medieval wall paintings in the county, and some very good glass. The wall painting depicts Cain and Abel, and survives in the deep splay of a south window. Cain holds a wheatsheaf and Abel a lamb. It dates from the Norman period and was discovered under whitewash in 1908. To the east is a small window at the same height constructed in Tudor times to throw light on to the rood figures. It contains fragments of early glass. In the quatrefoils of the north windows are fourteenth-century painted figures of the seated Christ and the Virgin and Child. A modern addition to the furnishings is the wooden font, which was given in 1975.

WEST MALLING, St Mary the Virgin

A story of all's well that ends well. A Norman tower and thirteenth-century chancel are linked by a twentieth-century nave that replaced one erected in the eighteenth century. The work of these three periods blends together very well and is enhanced by some good fittings. The west window and those in the south aisle are by Kempe and Tower, and of special note is the one depicting the Three Kings. On the south side of the chancel, backing on to a medieval lean-to vestry, is the splendid tomb of Sir Robert Brett (d. 1620), which has recently been restored. The colours are superb and show how churches must have looked when these monuments were new. In the north aisle is a large painting of the Last Supper by Francis Slater, the eighteenth-century artist who painted the ceilings of nearby Mereworth Castle. Hanging on the front of the west gallery are the Royal Arms of James II, of carved and painted wood. The twentieth-century rebuilding of the church was financed by the sale of an Elizabethan stoneware jug (now in the British Museum), the transaction being recorded on an inscribed stone in the north porch.

WEST PECKHAM, St Dunstan

Saxo-Norman, with a good early double-splayed window on the south face of the tower. The church is small, dark and welcoming, dating in the greater

WEST MALLING. The signature of Kempe and Tower in a south aisle window. If it were by Kempe alone, before 1907, it would not display a tower in the wheatsheaf symbol.

part from the fourteenth century. The north chapel contains the private pew of the Geary family. When the burial vault beneath became full the floor of the pew was raised by 8 ft to provide more burial space, creating a solid-floored galleried pew! It is panelled and benched and appears to be of expensive construction. However, closer inspection reveals that it is made of cheap wood grained and painted to look like oak! On the ceiling of the pew is a good collection of hatchments, and the top of the medieval monuments, lost when the floor was raised, may still be seen. Behind the altar is a series of continental wooden statues representing the Twelve Apostles which were a gift from Mereworth Castle. The chancel screen is twentieth century in date, and although it is a good example of craftsmanship is patently the wrong size – its loft is far too high for the medieval door opening that still survives in the north wall!

WEST STOURMOUTH, All Saints

The exterior is interesting for the little white bell turret at the west end is held up by two massive brick buttresses – a most extraordinary and unique construction. The interior is of great charm. The nave is filled with dark box pews which, under the west end, rise to an enormous height with poppy-heads of amazing richness. The floor is of red tiles – very uneven – and above are text boards of the eighteenth century. There is a colourful little organ near the chancel arch, and the base of the rood screen left in situ when its top was cut off at the Reformation.

WESTWELL, St Mary

A particularly rewarding church which throughout the Middle Ages belonged to Christ Church, Canterbury, which spent large sums of money on it. The chancel, by far the most elaborate part of the building, is separated from the nave by a screen of three trefoil arches supported on very tall cylindrical pillars. That this was *not* the rood screen may be seen by the notches cut into it that originally carried the wooden screen set in between. The chancel is vaulted in stone, held together today by essential iron tie-bars. The sedilia, of three seats, set under battlements, are unusual in having the two easternmost seats on the same level, with the third a few inches lower. The east window contains some medieval glass depicting the Tree of Jesse, while in the north chapel is some heraldic glass of Richard II's reign. There are some plain poppy-head stalls in the arcaded panels. In 1967 two flagons were sold to the Goldsmiths' Company to raise money for essential repairs to save this church from total collapse.

WICKHAMBREUX, St Andrew

The interior of this very pretty church is dominated by nineteenth-century work. The whole of the chancel and baptistry is lined with dark brown encaustic tiles, hiding a basically fourteenth-century church. The east window is an early example of American Art Nouveau in England, and dominates the entire building. It was designed by Baron Arild Rosenkrantz in 1896. Above the window are stencilled paintings of angels ascending, which can also be seen in the nave, while the roof there has a charming star-spangled sky. At the south-west corner is a vestry – screened off by an eighteenth-century screen which may have formed part of the refitting of the chancel paid for by Mary Young. Her monument in the chancel records that 'infirm from her youth she protracted life to the 68th year of her age'. She left £100 for wainscotting and ornamenting the chancel. The interior viewed from the east gives an unusual appearance as the aisles flank the tower (see also Sandhurst).

WILMINGTON, *St Michael and All Angels*

A very pretty church with a short spire. It was so rebuilt by Christian in the nineteenth century and Marchant in the early twentieth century, that it lacks character, but not interest. The base of the tower is undoubtedly Saxon and shows two double splayed windows that had been lost by infilling before the 1879 restoration. The large tub font is also probably Saxon, but has been smoothed over, having been used as a seat in the churchyard in the nineteenth century! The pulpit is of carved wood and is dated 1655 – a rare item as it is of the Commonwealth period. Its little pilaster buttresses that form each side of every panel taper very quickly and are pleasing to the eye. The piscina in the chancel was originally a holy water stoup and was discovered by Christian and adapted for its new use. The excellent wooden screen, with its Arts and Crafts detailing, was designed by Marchant and erected in 1920. The Royal Arms are those of George II. In the churchyard, by the doorway, is the tomb of Sir Edward Hulse (d. 1759), one of only three in England to have been designed by a Danish sculptor, Lawrence Anderson Holme, who came to England in 1762. His other two monuments are both at Axbridge in Somerset.

WINGHAM, *St Mary*

An enormous church, picturesquely set at an angle of the village street. It owes its size to the fact that it supported a college of priests in the Middle Ages. During the sixteenth century it was rebuilt, but the north aisle was demolished, reducing the church to the odd shape we see today. The unusual pillars which divide the nave from the south aisle are of timber, not stone. At the end of the south aisle is the Oxenden chapel, which contains their excellent bull's head monument. The metalwork screens and black and white pavements add great dignity to this part of the building. By going through a curved passage from the chapel you can emerge in the chancel, which is dominated by a stone reredos of fifteenth-century date. This French construction was a gift to the church in the 1930s and while it is not good quality carving, is an unusual find in a Kent church.

WINGHAM. In the south chapel is this wonderful memorial to the Oxenden family, erected in the late seventeenth century. The wrought-iron screen which closes this chapel is of the same date.

WITTERSHAM, *St John the Baptist*

An impressive church of mainly fourteenth-century date. The tower, which was still under construction in the early sixteenth century, is one of the most striking features. Externally it is memorable for the composition of the west door and window. The doorway has finely carved spandrels and label-stops, but the window above has two designs incorporated into it – Tudor arches for the bottom four lights, and Perpendicular arches above. It is quite a thing and obviously the result of local designs dying hard! On top of the tower is an excellent weathervane dated 1751. Inside, the tower arch is also memorable, a tall much-moulded feature; it is almost as impressive as the tower arch at Horsmonden. The north aisle shows evidence of rebuilding – the two octagonal pillars of fourteenth-century form replaced circular pillars, one of which survives. The church is very light, the east window containing only plain glass, which helps us to appreciate the furnishings and memorials of mainly twentieth-century date. In the south aisle is a tablet to Alfred Lyttleton (d. 1913), which was probably carved by Eric Gill. The interesting reredos of the high altar dates from 1967 and depicts St John the Baptist baptising Christ in a local river.

WOODCHURCH, *All Saints*

An enormous church with much of interest. The fabric dates from the thirteenth century, and the nave arcades of alternate round and octagonal piers are made of ragstone, which was polished in the nineteenth century to resemble Bethersden marble. In fact there are some genuine pieces of Bethersden marble in the church, particularly the shafts between the east window lancets. On the south-east buttress of the chancel is a mass dial, and on the main south wall is an excellent large sundial. The rood loft stairway survives in the north chapel where there is an excellent and rare double hagioscope. The sedilia are three graduated thirteenth-century constructions, with a good double piscina as part of the same scheme. In the south aisle is a medallion of the Blessed Virgin Mary, while the nearby east window which depicts the Crucifixion is by Kempe. In front of the pulpit is the brass to Nicholas Gore (d. 1333), a quatrefoil with a circular inscription, into which is set the figure of Gore in his vestments. The Royal Arms are those of George III and were painted by a local artist, Joseph Gibson, in 1773.

WOODNESBOROUGH, St Mary the Virgin

The tower makes this church one of the easiest in Kent to identify. It is capped by a little cupola and wooden balustrade of eighteenth-century date that replaced a medieval spire. During the Middle Ages the church was owned by Leeds Priory which invested heavily in the structure, and was no doubt responsible for the excellent sedilia built in about 1350. The canopy is supported by a quadripartite vault in turn supported by angry little heads. Above the sedilia is the cut-off end of a prickett beam. The east window, of Decorated style stonework, has a thirteenth-century hangover in the form of a shafted rere-arch. There are two excellent modern stained glass windows designed by F.W. Cole, which show the Creation (1980) and St Francis (1992). The good altar rails are of Queen Anne's reign, as are the recently restored Royal Arms.

WOULDHAM, All Saints

Famous for the grave of Walter Burke, in whose arms Nelson died. The church is low and visually undistinguished, but external appearances are misleading as it contains a great deal of interest. Part of the arcade between south aisle and nave is formed of Saxon walling, with a double splayed window visible over the central arch. The wall was cut through by the present arcade in the thirteenth century. There is a standard twelfth-century font of five columns supporting a square bowl. The tower stands in an unusual position to the north-west of the nave, and the doorway between tower and north aisle shows deep notches cut by the bell ropes when the small sanctus bell was tolled. By standing outside the door the ringer could see the high altar and the altar of St Blaise in the south chapel. A lancet in the chancel forms a low side window, while a more conventional, although much smaller, low side window exists in the south-east corner of the south aisle. There is also a fine fourteenth-century piscina.

WROTHAM, St George

In an excellent position overlooking the diminutive village square, the church is much larger than one imagines. It is entered under a two-storey stone-vaulted porch. On the right, inside the church, is a holy water stoup. The south chapel shows the rood loft staircase leading to a fourteenth-century screen. The altar in the chapel was designed by Comper in 1907. The stonework of the main east window was inserted in 1958 and came from St

Albans church in London, damaged in the Second World War. By far the best thing about Wrotham church is the chunky nineteenth-century stone and marble pulpit designed by Newman and Billing in 1861. The tower has an unusual feature – a vaulted passage leading right under it from north to south, to allow medieval processions to circumnavigate the building. There is nothing else like it in Kent!

WYE, *St Gregory and St Martin*

A very strange church, the result of the collapse of a tall central tower in 1686. The nave of the medieval church survives almost intact, while the chancel has been constructed from the remains of the central crossing of the thirteenth-century church, and a new tower built. The nave is tall and light, and contrasts well with the short narrow apsed chancel that now contains mural tablets to the Sawbridge and Drax families who lived at Olantigh. The

WYE. The nave of a medieval collegiate church of some size. The tower stands on the site of the former south transept and dates from a rebuilding of the early eighteenth century.

147

reredos is plain early eighteenth-century work and ties in nicely with the dark oak panelling. The choir stalls which stand in the nave were a thanksgiving memorial for the life of President Kennedy. The west window, which represents Christ in Majesty, is set into plain glass and was designed by Gerald Smith in the 1950s. It is an object lesson in how good glass of this period could be.

YALDING, Sts Peter and Paul

The little cupola on the west tower is topped by a weathervane dated 1734, and summons us to a large church, heavily restored in the 1860s, but worth travelling a long way to see. The nave roof has two interesting features – one is a sort of canopy of honour over the third bay from the west. It must have served some long-forgotten purpose. At the east end of the nave there is a real canopy of honour over the chancel arch. The south transept contains many interesting features – niches in the walls, bare stonework walls and a good arcaded tomb chest recessed into the south wall. There is a telling string course that suggests a thirteenth-century date, although the two windows in its east wall are Decorated in style. The most recent feature in the church – and by far the most important – is the engraved glass window in the chancel. It was engraved by Laurence Whistler in 1979 and commemorates Edmund Blunden, the First World War poet. It depicts a trench, barbed wire, a shell-burst and verses from Blunden's poems. This feature apart it is the nineteenth-century work that dominates Yalding – especially the awful encaustic tiles with arrow-like designs, the crude pulpit with symbols of the evangelists and the poor quality pews. The glass isn't much better, the Light of the World in the south chancel window being especially poor, but the south window of the south transept (1877) showing scenes from the Life of Christ redeems the state of the art.

Bibliography

Place of publication given only if it is outside London.

Betjeman, John. *Collins Guide to English Parish Churches*, Collins, 1968

Bignall, Alan. *The Kent Village Book*, Newbury, Countryside Books, 1986

Boorman, H.R.P. *Kent Churches*, Maidstone, Kent Messenger, 1954

Glynne, Sir S.R. *Notes on the Churches of Kent*, Murray, 1877

Grayling, F. *The Churches of Kent*, George Allen and Co., 1913

Homan, Roger. *The Victorian Churches of Kent*, Chichester, Phillimore, 1984

Jones, Lawrence. *Enjoying Historic Churches*, John Baker, 1964

Kemp, Brian. *English Church Monuments*, Batsford, 1980

Mee, Arthur. *The King's England – Kent*, Hodder and Stoughton, 1936

Newman, John. *Buildings of England, West Kent and the Weald*, Harmondsworth, Penguin, 1969

———. *Buildings of England, North-east and East Kent*, Harmondsworth, Penguin, 1969

Oyler, T. *The Parish Churches of the Diocese of Canterbury*, Hunter and Longhurst, 1910

Powys, A.R. *The English Parish Church*, Longmans Green and Co., 1930

Pritchard, V. *English Medieval Graffiti*, Cambridge, Cambridge University Press, 1967

Rodwell, W. *Our Christian Heritage*, George Philip, 1984

Smetham, H. *Rambles Round Churches* (4 vols), Parrett and Neves, 1925

Syms, J.A. *Kent Country Churches* (3 vols), Meresborough Books, 1984, 1987, 1989

Tricker, Roy. *County Guide to English Churches*, Newbury, Countryside Books, 1992

Wakeham, H. *The History of the Church of England*, Rivingtons, 1914

Webb, B. *Exploring Old British Churches*, Vawser and Wiles, 1948

Index of Places, Artists and Architectural Terms

Entries in bold type denote main gazetteer entries; those in italic type denote illustrations.

151